BATIK

as a hobby

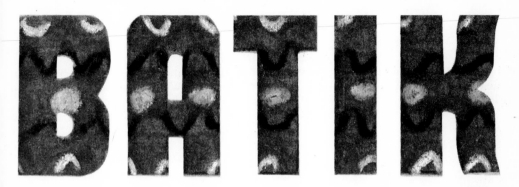

as a hobby

By VIVIAN STEIN

*Photographs and illustrations
by the author*

**STERLING
PUBLISHING CO., INC. NEW YORK**

Oak Tree Press Co., Ltd.
Distributed by WARD LOCK, Ltd., London & Sydney

DEDICATION
To Phil and Lisa

ACKNOWLEDGMENTS

All photographed batiks appearing on pages 76 to 79 are from the collection of the Los Angeles County Museum of Art. Illus. 89—bequest of Mrs. Leithead Wood; Illus. 90—gift of Harold Grieve; Illus. 92—gift of Mrs. Norman M. Kelly.

SOURCES OF SUPPLY

Tjantings and frames: Art supply dealers.

Alcohol lamp: Laboratory or art supply dealers.

Denatured alcohol: Drug stores or laboratory supply dealers.

Cleaning solvents: Cleaners-and-dyers supplies distributors.

Dyes: Drug stores, variety stores, dyers supplies distributors.

Glacial acetic acid: Chemical or photography supply dealers.

Thermometers: Laboratory supply dealers, or cookware department of a shop.

Wax: Paraffin—available in grocery stores, canning department.

Beeswax—check sewing notions department of a department store, or hardware stores, or art supply stores.

Third Printing, 1971

Copyright © 1969 by
Sterling Publishing Co., Inc.
419 Park Avenue South, New York 10016
British edition published by Oak Tree Press Co., Ltd.
Distributed in Great Britain and the Commonwealth by
Ward Lock, Ltd., 116 Baker Street, London W1
Manufactured in the United States of America
All rights reserved
Library of Congress Catalog Card No.: 69-19491
ISBN 0-8069-5132-8   UK 7061 2158 9
5133-X

CONTENTS

Color plates follow page 48

BEFORE YOU BEGIN

Batik-making offers you an opportunity to be creative while using simple materials. With wax, dye, and cloth, you can make beautiful decorated fabrics for wall hangings, pillow covers, draperies, screen dividers, or other uses. Batiks are made by painting or drawing a design with wax on cloth, dyeing the cloth, then removing the wax. A contrasting design is created because the parts that were covered with wax are not dyed. The cloth may be rewaxed and dyed several times in order to make intricate designs with many colors.

Batik employs what is known as a "resist" technique; the wax is used to resist the dye. Since wax is brittle when cold, the wax design often cracks when the cloth is handled. Dye seeps into the cracks, making a web-like design known as crackle, which is characteristic of batik. Crackle can be controlled to cover only a portion of the design, or it may cover the entire piece, adding dimension and depth to the design.

Traditionally, smooth fabrics, such as muslin, broadcloth, or silk have been used for batik, because the close weave takes fine detail and the wax penetrates completely through the cloth. By using different types of fabrics, however, you can create unique and interesting effects. Coarse or heavy fabrics add interesting texture to wall hangings. Sheer fabrics can be waxed while folded to make "repeat" patterns, ones in which the design is repeated although drawn only once. These patterns are appropriate for curtains or dress material. Piled fabrics such as corduroy and velveteen make interesting wall hangings. Because of the thickness of the fabric and the depth of the pile, color can be built up in layers, creating an effect like a painting.

There are many ways to make a batik. You can use your imagination to experiment with different fabrics and ways of applying wax. Since you are working with liquid wax, you may be very spontaneous and draw much of the design directly on the cloth. If you accidentally drip wax, incorporate the resulting dots into the design. You can scratch fine lines into the wax with a stylus and make wide lines with a brush.

Part of the enjoyment of batik comes from

Illus. 1. This batik wall hanging of an angel was made by painting the wax on with a brush and then painting the individual dyes on.

the surprise of experimentation. What will you see when the wax is removed? Even though you may have planned every step carefully, it is still hard, when the project is thickly covered with wax, to imagine what it will look like when it is dyed. Your first look at the finished batik is an exciting moment.

You will make a series of projects which will introduce you to the tools and techniques of batik-making. Each project will add to your knowledge of the creative possibilities of this ancient craft. Step-by-step directions and patterns are given for each project, but you are encouraged to add your own touches and experiment with the techniques you learn.

Each project tells you the special materials required, but there are a few basic materials you will use in all the projects.

WAX

Many types of wax mixtures can be used successfully in batik-making. The two most commonly used waxes are paraffin and beeswax. The batik wax that art dealers supply is usually a mixture of the two.

Paraffin is more brittle than beeswax, and is especially useful if crackle is desired. You can obtain it in grocery stores in the form of blocks for use in preserving jellies. A dye bath up to 90 degrees F. can be used with paraffin.

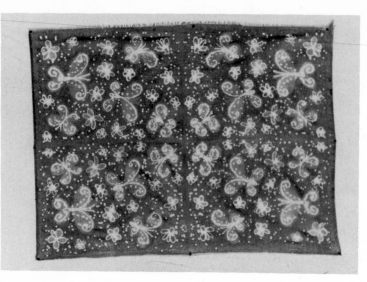

Illus. 2. A scarf with a repeat design was made by folding the sheer fabric in half twice before waxing and dyeing.

Beeswax is more flexible than paraffin, doesn't crack as easily, and can take a higher temperature dye bath, up to 110 degrees F. This is an advantage, as colors take faster in a hotter dye bath than in a cool one. Beeswax is sold as dressmaker's beeswax, or is sometimes available in hardware stores. A commonly used mixture of beeswax and paraffin is three parts beeswax to two parts paraffin, or you may use equal amounts of each. These mixtures result in a fairly flexible wax that is not as expensive as pure beeswax. If you do not want crackle, use a mixture or pure beeswax.

HEAT SOURCE AND CONTAINER FOR WAX

Wax may be melted in the top of a double boiler, in an electric frying pan, or in a pot, such as an empty coffee percolator, which allows easy pouring of the wax. You must be careful not to overheat the wax, or it may start smoking or catch fire. Either a hot plate or a stove burner covered with an asbestos pad is a good heat source. The asbestos pad prevents the flame or heat coil from coming in direct contact with the pot, lessening the danger of fire.

The wax should be heated to at least 170 degrees F. It should be stirred occasionally to hasten melting and to keep the wax from overheating. Often by the time the last piece of wax has melted, the liquid is too hot to use; it should be allowed to cool a little before waxing the batik. You can test it by waxing extra scraps of cloth.

While you are working, turn the heat off under the pot and reheat when necessary. Otherwise the wax may get too hot. Be very careful when handling the pot of wax. You could get a severe burn if it spills. Avoid getting any water near the wax container, as water in the wax may cause the wax to splatter out of the pot.

DYE BATH CONTAINERS

You need a small glass or china bowl to mix the powdered dye with very hot water. The concentrated liquid dye is then added to clear, lukewarm water in the dye bath container and mixed thoroughly before the batik is placed in it.

Dyeing may be done in a plastic or enamelled pan, or in the sink or bathtub if the piece is large. You should not use metal pans, as some metals tend to react with the dye.

Dye may permanently stain some plastics, and may stain the enamel of an old sink or bathtub if the surface is worn. The stains may be removed from enamel with bleaching cleanser, or by letting a solution of bleach and water stand in the tub until the stains are gone. Follow the directions on the bleach container.

The dye container should be large enough so that the batik may be fully immersed in the dye.

RUBBER GLOVES

Rubber gloves are useful for handling the batik while it is wet from the dye bath.

TONGS

Kitchen tongs are used to pick up the batik from the dye or from hot wax after the cloth has been dipped for crackling.

IRON AND PAPERS
FOR REMOVING WAX

Since wax and dye tend to clog the vents of a steam iron, it is better to have a plain electric iron for use in removing the wax from a batik. A steam iron is used after the wax is removed to set the dye and finish the piece.

You will also need newspapers to absorb the wax, and some unprinted absorbent paper to place next to the batik. Paper towels may be used for small batiks. Plain newsprint paper is good for larger batiks. This paper may be obtained as roll ends from newspaper printers, or in pads from an art supply store. The technique of removing the wax is discussed in the first project.

Ideally, you should have a work table and space for your tools near your hot plate or stove. If you cannot, you may set the pot of hot wax on a pot holder or asbestos pad near where you are working. It will stay hot a long time. In any case, the floor should be protected with newspapers, as wax drips are a nuisance to clean up.

FABRICS AND DYES

The project directions tell you the type of fabric to use and give instructions on how to use the dyes. Many of today's fabrics are

Illus. 3. Because of the pile of the corduroy, this owl wall hanging has the effect of a painting.

mixtures of synthetics and cotton. Synthetics do not dye well with most dyes, so you should avoid fabrics which contain dacron, nylon, etc. Check the label. Cotton and linen may be dyed with household dyes. Silk or synthetics must have special dyes. Commercial batik dyes are available and will be discussed later.

In addition to white cloth, which makes dye colors show up well, you may make batiks on colored cloth or prints. If you use colored cloth, use dyes that will contrast well. Printed fabrics using small stripes or floral patterns are suitable for a silhouette type of design, with a dark background that shows off the printed area. You may also combine batik with embroidery or appliqué.

Before you begin a project, the fabric must be prepared by washing it with detergent and water to remove all fillers and finishing materials which may interfere with dyeing. Rinse in water without using fabric softener, and let dry. Unless the project directions give further instructions, you may iron the cloth smooth, and begin the project.

In the check list of materials preceding each project, standard equipment such as dye bath containers, tongs, irons, etc. are not listed.

PROJECT ONE: CAN-DECORATED PLACE MATS

Materials
  white cotton cloth, 14 × 19 inches, un-
    hemmed, for each place mat
  empty cans of different sizes
  one package household dye
  pot holder
  dry-cleaning fluid (optional)
  white vinegar (optional)

Empty cans of various sizes are used as stamps to decorate a place mat for this first project. Batik fabrics made commercially in Indonesia today are stamped with very elaborate brass stamps to simulate hand-drawn batik. You will use simpler stamps, but the idea is the same.

You may use an all-cotton broadcloth, percale, or even an old sheet for this project. Since it is easy to make mistakes and spoil a cloth when you wax, it is better to wait until you are finished batiking before you hem the mat. By practicing first on an extra piece of cloth, you will learn the technique and should be able to stamp designs on the mats with little trouble. (See finished mats on color page C.)

Waxing is easiest when the cloth is laid flat. Lay the prepared cloth on newspapers, or cardboard, which you have covered with household waxed paper, available in grocery stores. The newspapers or cardboard act as insulation of the work surface and help keep the wax from cooling too rapidly as you work. The waxed paper keeps the batik from sticking to the work surface. If you find it difficult to see the wax design on the fabric, lay a sheet of colored paper beneath the waxed paper.

Completely remove the top of each can. Punch a hole in the closed end of each can, or remove that end, too. This allows air to escape when the can is dipped into the wax. Pick up a can with a pot holder and dip the

Illus. 4. Using a pot holder, dip the open end of the can into the melted wax for 30 seconds.

Illus. 5. After shaking off the excess wax, press the can on the cloth until liquid wax appears all around the rim of the can.

open end into the wax. Hold it so that just the rim of the can is covered with wax. Count 30 seconds to allow the metal to heat, then lift the can and tip it to shake off excess wax drops into the pot. Be careful not to splash the cloth. Quickly move the can over the cloth and press it until liquid wax appears all around the rim.

12

Illus. 6. Lift the can, leaving a ring of wax. Vary the size of the cans to add interest to the design on the place mat.

When you lift the can, you will see a circle of wax. Make a design of rings, using several different sizes of cans for variety. If you are careful, you can rewax a ring that is too thin by dipping the can in wax again and placing it on exactly the same spot.

If you make drips, you may either start over and work until you have a design that is smooth, or you may incorporate dots into the design by using a brush to drip wax all over the design, making a polka dot effect.

When you have finished the design, you are ready to dye the mat. Turn the batik over and peel the waxed paper from the cloth. Do not peel the cloth from the paper, as this will crack the wax on the batik.

One package of dye will dye about 3 yards of material. If you have several mats to dye, you can use the whole package; if not, just use part of a package. The color should contrast well with the white design, so you should choose a bright color such as red, blue, green, or gold. Don't use black or navy blue; these colors do not work well in cool water.

Check the dye package for special directions. Household dyes usually employ only hot water. Our directions are slightly different, as we will use lukewarm water. Heat two cups of water until bubbles begin to form; then add the dye to it. The solution will be about 190 degrees F. Stir to mix thoroughly. Strain the concentrated dye through a wet cloth into the dye bath container. Fill the container with enough lukewarm water (80–90 degrees F.) to cover the material. Unless the package directions of the dye advise differently, add 1 tablespoon un-iodized salt to each gallon of liquid, or 1 teaspoon to the quart, to act as a dye fixative.

Wet the place mat with lukewarm water before immersing it in the dye bath you have prepared. Move it gently every few minutes to keep the dye circulating, and check the color frequently. When wet, the batik looks about twice as dark as it will look when it is dry. When the place mat is the right color, remove it from the bath with tongs or rubber gloves, and rinse it in lukewarm water until

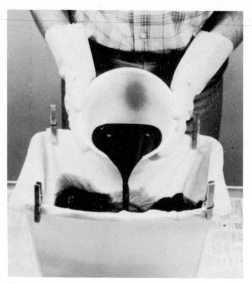

Illus. 7. Strain concentrated dye through a wet cloth into a container of lukewarm water. Mix to form the dye bath.

the water runs clear. Do not squeeze or wring the cloth; if you do, the wax will crack. Save the dye until the batik is dry. If the color is too light, you can rewet the cloth and dye it again until the color is right.

Let the place mat dry thoroughly. Hang it so it will stay smooth and flat. Do not dry batik in the direct sun. The wax may melt and run onto the wet dye.

After the place mat is dry, you are ready to remove the wax. Place a heavy layer of newspapers on an ironing board, with a layer of plain absorbent paper on top. Lay the batik on the absorbent paper, cover it with another layer of absorbent paper, then a final layer of newspapers. If you don't use plain paper next to the batik, ink from the newspapers may transfer on to the cloth.

Run an iron, set one setting lower than the type of fabric used, over the papers covering the place mat. As the wax melts, it soaks into

Illus. 8. Dip the wet batik into the dye bath and move gently until the color is correct. Handle the cloth with rubber gloves or a pair of tongs.

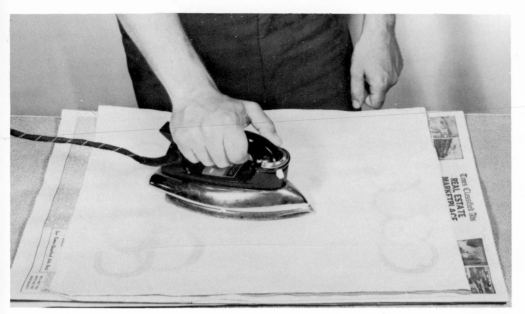

Illus. 9. After the batik is dry, iron the wax out on to layers of absorbent papers. The newspaper layer has been left off the top to show you how the wax is absorbed by the paper.

the papers, which you discard and replace with fresh papers, both on top and on the bottom, until no more wax is absorbed from the cloth. (After most of the wax is absorbed, you can dispense with the top layer of newspaper, but not with any of the other layers of paper.)

After ironing, you will notice that some wax has been absorbed by the cloth around the previously waxed area, making the area darker than the surrounding cloth. To get rid of the wax ring, the batik must be cleaned in a solvent. You may take your place mats to a professional dry-cleaner, or clean them yourself.

If you clean the mats yourself, we suggest you use a non-flammable solvent such as "Valclene"* or "Perclene"* or the equiva-

* Registered DuPont trademark.

lent, which are available through distributors of supplies to the dry-cleaning trade. Since these distributors sell materials wholesale, you may have to buy several gallons at a time, but these solvents are much safer to use than the flammable solvents readily available. You may also wish to check with a dry-cleaning plant to see if they might sell solvent.

Flammable solvents which remove wax are white gasoline, available at some auto service stations, and naphtha benzene, available at chemical supply dealers. These solvents must be used out of doors, away from heat or any flame such as a pilot light, as the fumes may ignite and explode. *Do not smoke* while using any solvent, and work in a well-ventilated area.

Pour the solvent into a bowl, and immerse the batik. Squeeze gently until the stiffness

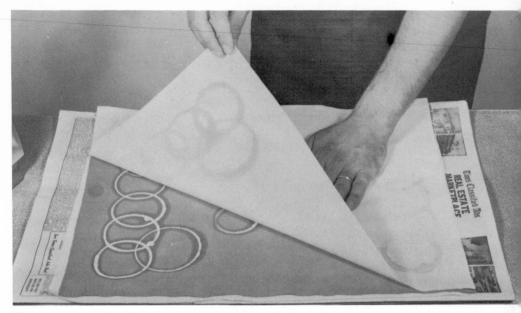

Illus. 10. Wax is absorbed by both the paper and the cloth surrounding the waxed area. To remove the wax completely, the cloth must be dry-cleaned.

is gone, and hang the mat up to dry. After cleaning several mats, or if you have a batik with a great deal of wax, you may need to discard the old solvent and start again with a fresh solution.

When the mat is dry, and the solvent smell is gone, lay a cloth soaked in white vinegar over the batik, and steam iron it to set the dye. Hem the mat, and press with an iron to finish it. If the surface or color doesn't seem smooth enough, use spray sizing available in grocery stores, to add a finish. Follow the directions on the can. The use of vinegar is optional because the fumes are unpleasant. However, it does help to set household dyes, which tend to fade in time even when salt is added as a fixative.

Illus. 11. The completed place mat has a simple ring design where it was stamped with wax.

16

Illus. 12. For variety of design, use cookie cutters to stamp the wax on to the cloth. Hold the cookie cutter with pliers.

When the mats get dirty, dry-clean them. If you wash them, use a mild detergent and separate them from other articles in case the dye bleeds.

As a variation, cookie cutters may also be used to stamp designs. In addition to the materials used for the other mats, you will need cookie cutters with handles and a pair of pliers. The pliers are used to grip the handle of the cookie cutter when it is dipped into the hot wax and stamped on the cloth. Dip the cutter in the wax for about 25 seconds, shake off the excess wax, and stamp the cutter on the cloth. The rest of the procedure is the same as for the can place mat.

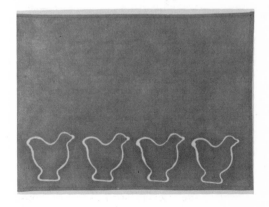

Illus. 13. The cookie-cutter design on this place mat resulted in a parade of chickens along the bottom.

PROJECT TWO: BRUSH DESIGN
PILLOW

Materials
two 15 × 15-inch squares of cotton cloth
two packages household dye
bristle brushes
cleaning fluid (optional)
pillow stuffing

Use a finely-woven cotton cloth such as percale, muslin, or broadcloth for your pillows. The illustrated pillows (see color page C) were made from old, percale sheets. Wash the fabric; then cut it into squares. You should have two pieces of cloth for each pillow. You may wax both cloths to make a design on both sides of the pillow, or wax only one for the front of the pillow. The back can be dyed in the last dye bath to match the color of the front. Directions are given for waxing one cloth. To batik both sides, repeat each step for the second cloth.

Two colors of dye are needed. Suggested color combinations are turquoise and green, yellow and brown, or pink and red.

Stiff bristle brushes such as oil or house painting brushes are suitable for applying the wax. Brushes about 1 to 2 inches wide are

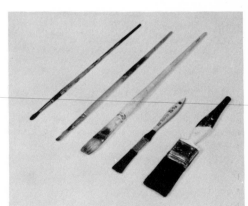

Illus. 14. A variety of stiff, bristle brushes may be used to apply the wax.

useful for filling in large areas. Smaller lines may be made by using the narrow side of a

Illus. 15. Place the cloth on newspaper and waxed paper. Paint the wax on in abstract swirls.

flat brush, or by trimming the bristles to a point with scissors or a razor. A ½-inch wide nylon house painting brush was used to make the illustrated pillows.

Bristles made of animal hair may get singed in the hot wax. It is better to buy quality brushes with synthetic bristles. Cheap watercolor brushes will not hold their shape in hot wax, and are useless.

When you are ready to wax, lay the washed and ironed cloth on newspapers covered with waxed paper. Dip the brush into the hot wax, then press it against the side of the pot to squeeze out the excess wax. Try making an abstract design by painting a few swirling strokes on different parts of the cloth. The wax should be hot enough to penetrate the cloth with each brush stroke. If the wax has

gone through the cloth properly, the area will look wet. Work quickly, allowing the brush to miss a few spots, as this will add texture to the finished batik.

Cover a few areas with brush strokes, and let the wax drip or splash in spots to add to the design. Everything covered with wax now will stay white. Leave enough cloth unwaxed to allow for the next two colors.

When you are through using the brush, press the excess wax out against the side of the pot, and lay the brush on waxed paper to cool with the wax still in it. Be careful not to bend the wax-laden bristles after they cool, as they could be easily broken.

After the batik has cooled, turn it over and peel the waxed paper from the cloth. Check the back to see that wax has gone through in

19

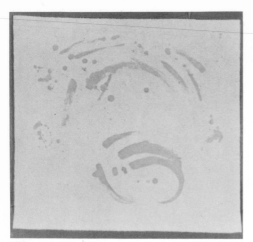

Illus. 16. The areas waxed now will remain white. The cloth is ready for its first dye bath—turquoise.

all the spots you want to remain completely white. If an area seems too thin, lay the cloth on waxed paper and rewax the back. The batik is now ready for the first dye bath, which will be the lighter of the two colors you have chosen.

Dissolve the dye in hot water, and mix it with the lukewarm dye bath as in Project One. Wet the batik and immerse it in the dye. When the color looks right to you, remove the batik, and rinse it until the water runs clear, then hang it up to dry. Be careful about drying it in the direct sunlight. If the sun is too hot, the wax will melt. Also, do not use a drier or iron to hasten drying, or you will melt the wax, which must remain on the cloth throughout the second dyeing.

When the batik is dry, you are ready for the second waxing. After the wax is hot, set the brush in the pot until the solidified wax in the brush melts again. Proceed as before, brushing wax on the colored areas you want to save. You should also rewax any white areas where the wax is cracked, thin, or peeling.

Prepare the second dye bath as before. If the dye pan is stained from the first bath, clean it with bleaching cleanser to remove the

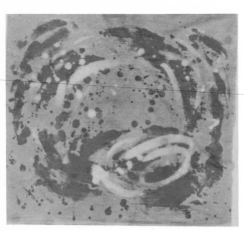

Illus. 17. After the cloth was dyed turquoise, more wax was splashed on. The newly waxed areas will remain turquoise.

Illus. 18. Next the batik was dyed dark green, which makes the turquoise and white areas stand out. (See color page C.)

Illus. 19. Instead of an abstract design, try a heart-shaped pattern. First wax the white cloth as shown. Prepare a pink dye bath.

Illus. 20. This is what the cloth looks like after being dyed pink. The waxed areas will remain white.

old dye. Let the batik cool, peel off the waxed paper, and dye as you did the first time.

After the batik is dry, you may remove the wax completely, or you may dip it in wax a final time, if you do not want to use cleaning

solvents. When you dip the batik in a final coating of wax so all areas are covered, you merely iron the wax out, without using cleaning solvents. The batik will be slightly stiff, but the colors will be about as bright

Illus. 21. Wax additional areas (the dark surfaces in the photo) to complete the design. They will stay pink in the next dyeing.

Illus. 22. The batik is next dyed red and the wax removed by ironing and dry-cleaning. (See color page C for finished pillow.)

21

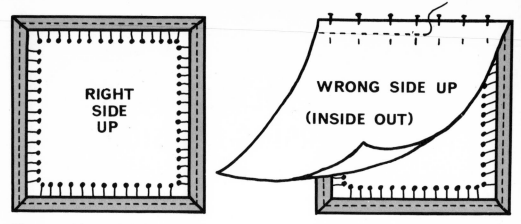

Illus. 23. With one cloth facing right side up, sew the fringe all around as shown in the diagram on the left. Place the second cloth facing wrong side up over the first and sew the two cloths together making sure the tape of the fringe is outside the seam line as in the diagram at the right.

and dark as they were when the dye was wet. There will be no wax rings around the brush strokes, because the background will have a wax coating also.

If you want the fabric to be softer, iron the wax out after the second dyeing, without dipping the entire batik in wax. There will be wax rings around the brush strokes. To remove these, dip the ironed batik in cleaning fluid until all stiffness is gone. After the cleaning fluid has evaporated and the smell is gone, steam iron the batik with or without vinegar to set the dye. Use spray sizing if desired. Starch may be used instead.

To finish the pillow, place the two squares together inside out; sew three sides together and part of the fourth, leaving a hole for stuffing. Turn the material right side out, stuff, and hand-sew the opening shut.

To add a fringe, lay one cloth right side up and place the fringe so that the tape edge meets the edge of the cloth, with the fringe pointing toward the middle of the cloth. Sew the tape in place along all four sides of the cloth. Lay the second cloth, inside out, over the fringe and sew through both layers of cloth and tape. Pin and sew each side separately, in order to shake the fringe toward the middle as you work. Sew three sides, and the corners of the fourth side, leaving a hole for stuffing. Turn right side out, stuff, and sew the opening shut.

The brush design does not have to be completely abstract, as is shown by the pillow cover using a heart design. You may make solid areas of color by painting a definite area with wax, rather than splashing it on.

SELECTING, ENLARGING, AND TRANSFERRING A DESIGN

Ideas for batik designs may be adapted from many sources. Embroidery patterns are particularly good, as are posters, illustrations or simple, abstract designs. Flat, two-dimensional designs are generally easier to do in batik than those giving the illusion of a three-dimensional picture. This is due to the nature of the translucent wax medium. When you draw in wax, it is just the opposite of drawing in pencil. The wax line is lighter than the surrounding background. This makes it difficult to draw shadows or objects showing depth.

Rather than trying to imitate drawings or oil paintings, take advantage of the nature of the wax by using crackled areas, or light lines on a dark background. By applying wax of different temperatures, and thick or thin layers of wax, you can obtain variations in texture and color.

For example, the pink areas of the heart pillow show a mottled pattern caused by thick and thin areas of wax. As the wax cooled on the brush, the brush strokes became thicker than when the first layer of hot wax was applied. Some spots were covered with two layers of wax. As a result, areas that had thicker layers of wax remained pink, while the thin layers of wax were penetrated somewhat by the red dye, giving a darker tint of pink.

In order to avoid any variation in texture, the velveteen hood in Project Nine was covered with three layers of wax, assuring a thick, even coating.

Generally, the hotter the wax, the thinner the layer it forms on the cloth. Very cool wax tends to remain on top of the fibres and not penetrate them at all. Unless the coating of wax is thick, dye will be absorbed. Thus, fabrics covered with only one layer of very hot or very cold wax will become tinted in whatever dye bath you use. You can employ this technique intentionally as in Project Three, where hot wax is used to leave the surface ends of the corduroy pile unwaxed and result in a tinted background.

When you have decided on a design idea, sketch it on graph paper to make enlarging easier. In addition, it is often helpful to have a color sketch to refer to if you have a complex design. You may also want to list or diagram the steps of waxing and dyeing a complicated design.

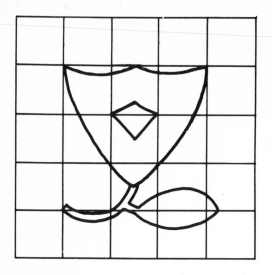

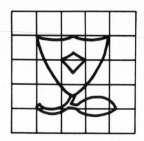

Illus. 24. The smaller diagram represents the original design which has been marked off into squares. To enlarge the pattern, a bigger grid of an equal number of squares is drawn and each line of the design is drawn in exactly as it appears in the corresponding small square.

HOW TO ENLARGE A DESIGN

A design can be drawn free-hand on the fabric with pencil, charcoal, or blackboard chalk (not tailor's chalk), or if you prefer, you can make a small sketch, then enlarge the design on paper, and transfer it to the fabric.

To enlarge a design, first draw a grid of uniform squares across your sketch, using a ruler and a pencil. Make the squares any suitable size. It is convenient to draw your original sketch on graph paper, which is marked in squares, saving you the trouble of ruling them yourself.

Draw the same number of squares on your pattern paper as you have on the sketch. For example, you may have 40 squares on the sketch. There should be 40 correspondingly large squares on the pattern paper. You can enlarge the sketch to any size. If your sketch is 10 squares wide, you can mark the pattern paper with 10 1-inch squares across it to make a batik 10 inches wide. Or you can mark a pattern paper with 10 2-inch squares

across it to make a batik 20 inches wide. The length of the pattern can be determined by the number of squares in one vertical column on the sketch. A vertical column of 10 squares enlarged to 10 1-inch squares will give you a batik 10 inches in length.

After drawing the squares, in each large square on the pattern paper, copy the portion of the design exactly as it appears in the same square on the smaller sketch. When you have completed the drawing, the pattern is ready to be transferred to the fabric.

Each pattern in this book is drawn so that one square represents a 1-inch square. Rule your pattern into 1-inch squares, then enlarge from the pattern in the book. The squares are numbered to help you locate each section easily.

TRANSFERRING THE DESIGN

You may transfer the design onto the cloth by placing the pattern under the cloth, taping both to a window and tracing the

24

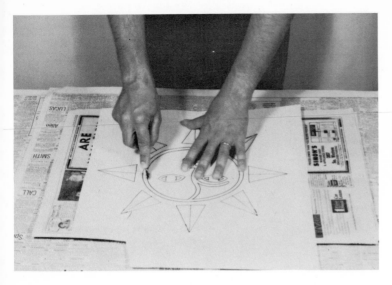

Illus. 25. To transfer a design by the powder method, score holes in the paper pattern with a tracing wheel.

lines of the pattern. To make tracing easier, first go over the lines of the pattern with a felt tip pen. The thick dark line shows up well underneath the cloth. You may also cut out the design elements, lay them on the cloth, and trace around them.

Pencil lines may show on the finished batik if you are using light-colored dyes, but most of the time pencil or charcoal is satisfactory to use.

If you cannot trace the design, it may be transferred by means of a tracing wheel,

Illus. 26. With the cloth laid underneath the pattern, rub powdered charcoal or colored talcum into the scored holes.

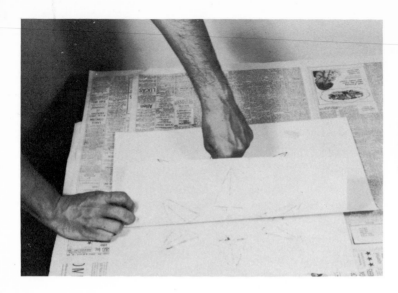

Illus. 27. The powder
shows up on the cloth
as a series of dots,
transferring the design.

which punches a series of holes in the
pattern. Lay the pattern on a soft surface
such as a smooth rug or a heavy pad of
newspapers, and run a dressmaker's or
draftsman's tracing wheel around the outlines of the pattern. Lay the punched pattern
on the cloth. Powdered charcoal, draftsman's
pouncing powder, or colored talcum may
then be rubbed through the holes, transferring the design.

Talcum powder can be colored by mixing
it with liquid food coloring. After it dries,
crush it with a spoon to make a powder
again.

PROJECT THREE: "PARTRIDGE IN A PEAR TREE" WALL HANGING

Materials
    white cotton corduroy, 18 × 24 inches
    dyes—red, yellow, green, brown
    No. 10 flat oil painting brush
    flat ½-inch wide brush
    four one-quart jars
    small glass or china bowls
    waxed paper
    newspapers
    paper towels

Materials for framing
    two pieces moulding or half rounds,
        20 inches long for top frame
    fringe, or two more pieces of moulding for
        bottom frame
    two pieces black twill tape, each 3 inches
        long
    two pot holder or drapery rings
    small finishing nails
    carpet tacks or stapler
    paint

With hot wax and a little patience, you can make an interesting batik that resembles a tapestry. (See color page A.) Most of the waxing is simple. You fill in the background with wax, leaving a stencil-like design which you paint with dyes.

The corduroy used for the illustrated batik had six wales or ribs to the inch. You can also use the standard, finer corduroy if the wide wale is unavailable. When you transfer the design to the corduroy, make sure the pile runs toward the top of the design. Brush the cloth to feel the direction in which the pile runs. The cloth feels smooth when your hand brushes in the same direction as the pile runs, and it feels rough when your hand brushes against the pile. The pile causes an optical effect with colors appearing darker

or lighter depending on the way the light strikes the pile. With the usual overhead lighting, a wall hanging looks best if the pile runs upward. If the pile runs toward the bottom of the wall hanging, light is reflected off the threads and the color appears washed out. (See Illus. 29.)

Lay the corduroy on newspapers covered with several sheets of waxed paper. While you are waxing, keep the wax hot the entire time, in order for it to go through the thick cloth. Use the No. 10 oil painting brush to wax the complete design. The smaller brush is used to paint on dyes.

Dip the brush in the hot wax; then press out excess wax against the side of the pot. Hold the brush so the flat side is parallel to the outline of the design. Hold the handle

27

Illus. 28.

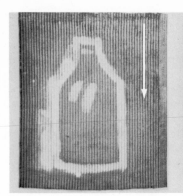

Illus. 29. These three samples were dyed exactly the same color and yet they appear different. This is because the pile of the corduroy runs in a different direction in each case. (The arrows show the direction.) When batiking on corduroy the best effect is obtained when the pile is running upward. Bear this in mind when you transfer the partridge pattern (opposite page) to your cloth.

upright and touch the bottom of the brush on the cloth close to the outline, until wax flows up to the line. Move the brush around the outline, keeping it parallel, rewaxing the brush whenever necessary. Daub the wax around all the outlines first; then fill in the background solidly with wax, when the outlining is finished

Outline the silhouette of the bird, but do not paint wax on the wing, leg, bill or eye. This is done after you have dyed the first color on the bird. Leave each entire leaf as well as the tree and pears unwaxed.

To wax the border, hold the brush upright, and paint a line of wax on the top and bottom of the border, using the same daubing technique used on the outlines. Allow an extra margin of cloth on the outer edges of the borders, to add the frame. Divide the border into squares. Paint the diagonals with the brush held upright. Make all the diagonals in one direction and let the wax cool completely before waxing diagonals in the other direction, to prevent the wax lines from

running together. When you are finished waxing, turn the batik over and rewax any areas on the back where the wax failed to penetrate the cloth fully. Don't wax any of the areas you plan to dye.

You may use household dyes, or com-

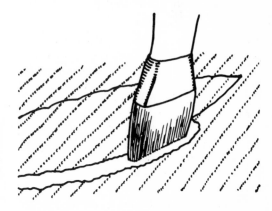

Illus. 30. To wax the background, hold the brush upright and parallel to the outline. Let wax flow up to the line.

29

Illus. 31. The background is waxed, leaving an unwaxed silhouette of the bird, tree, and pears, which are painted with dyes.

mercial batik dyes to dye your wall hanging. The advantage of batik dyes is they are made to be used in cool water, and tend to be more permanent or fadeproof than household dyes. Batik dyes come in powdered form, and should be mixed according to the manufacturer's directions. Add 1 tablespoon uniodized salt to each gallon of liquid batik dye, or 1 teaspoon to the quart, to act as a dye fixative just as you do with household dyes.

Mix a quart of each color in the jars. If you use household dyes, dissolve two-thirds of a package of dye in a quart of water. Since you will paint the dyes on, they need to be stronger than if you were going to dip the cloth in dye.

Try the dyes on a piece of scrap cloth that has been dampened and wrung dry, to test the strength of the colors. Add more dye powder if necessary, to make deep colors. Lighter colors are made by adding water to a portion of the dye.

The entire cloth may be wet before dyeing, or you may wet a section at a time with the small brush. In either case, lay the batik on waxed paper and blot excess water out of the unwaxed areas until they are just damp.

Dip a spoonful of each color of dye into a small dish. The red and yellow should be bright, full-strength colors. The basic brown and green should be fairly dark. Mix light green and light brown by adding water to the dark dyes in separate dishes. Test the colors on the scrap cloth until you have a pleasing effect. Remember the dry batik will be lighter than it is while wet.

Using the small brush, paint the upper and lower triangles in each border yellow. Paint each pear yellow. Shading is added later. Be careful not to paint any of the waxed area, as it may stain with a tint of color.

If the color appears too dark, blot the area with a paper towel to lift off the dye. You may blot the water out of areas that are too light and repaint them with dye to add more color. You will be rinsing the dyed areas later and will lose some color, so make all areas a little darker than the color you want. To make the shading on the pears, blot the pear dry with paper towels; then paint light brown along the left-hand edge of each pear, extending the shading across the bottom of the pear.

Paint the leaves light green. The tree trunk is light brown, shaded along each edge with dark brown. The brown dye will run into the bird if the area is wet. Blot the leg with a towel to lessen the chance the dye will run.

Illus. 32. Wax the bird's head and body after they are painted, but leave unwaxed areas for a bill, eye and wing. Wax half of each painted leaf. (Shaded areas represent wax.)

The central triangles of the border are red. If the bird, which is red, is painted immediately, the red dye will run into the tree branch. Let the batik dry completely and wax the branch before painting the bird. Shade the edges of the bird with brown.

After the first dyeing is complete, let the batik dry thoroughly to set the dye; then rinse out the excess dye. If you don't rinse out the excess dye well, it may dissolve in the melted wax during ironing, and stain the background. If any areas need retouching, blot dry, redye, then rinse. Let the batik dry again.

Wax the areas that are finished—the border, tree trunk, and pears. Cover half of each leaf with wax. Hold the brush upright along the middle line. Let the wax flow to the line, to form a straight line down the middle of the leaf. Fill in the remainder of the half leaf with wax.

Similarly, hold the brush upright and wax the bird's head and body, leaving unwaxed

areas for a bill, eye and wing. Leave the leg unwaxed.

Paint the unwaxed half of the leaves dark green; paint the wing, eye, bill and leg of the bird, dark brown. You can blot and redye the leaves and bird as many times as necessary to get the right color. Then let the batik dry to help set the dye; then rinse the excess dye out of the leaves and bird.

Let the batik dry thoroughly before the final waxing. Wax the leaves and bird, and go over the pears and tree trunk again to make sure they are completely covered with wax. Do not rewax the background.

Run cold water over the batik to chill the wax. Crack the wax by bending the batik

Illus. 33. The finished tree trunk and pears are waxed, as well as the red part of the bird's body and half of the light green leaves. Then the details of the bird are painted brown and the other half of each leaf is painted dark green.

31

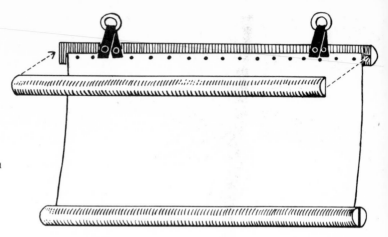

Illus. 34. Tack the batik to a strip of moulding. Attach rings for hanging. Cover with a second strip of moulding.

backwards diagonally and across, so there are a number of cracked places when you look at the back. Wipe off water drops from the front and back of the batik with towels; then reseal both the front and back of the bird, pear, and tree design with wax. It is not necessary to reseal the border.

Make a clear, lukewarm dye bath sufficiently large to cover the entire batik. Use the full-strength yellow and green dyes you have left in the jars and mix the contents of the two jars together. Warm the yellow-green dye and add it to the dye bath.

Wet the batik, then immerse it in the dye. The entire surface of the batik except the heavily waxed design will become tinted with color if you used hot wax to cover the background. This is because the wax sinks to the base of the pile, leaving the surface ends unwaxed. The ends pick up dye and are tinted, while the base remains free of dye.

After the color looks deep enough, rinse the batik, saving the dye. Most of the dye will rinse away from the surface, leaving only a tint. Redye and rinse until you are satisfied with the color.

After a final rinse, let the batik dry thoroughly before ironing the wax out. Iron with many changes of paper, and a heavy layer of paper underneath to protect the ironing board from absorbing wax. The batik will be stiff after ironing, even though the papers will no longer absorb wax. Since this is a wall hanging, it is not necessary to remove every trace of wax.

Trim any ravelled edges from the batik. The bottom may be finished by sewing on a fringe or braid, or with wood similar to the rod you will attach to the top for hanging. Use narrow moulding or standard lumber half rounds to form the rod or rods. Paint or stain the wood before you put the pieces together. Black, brown, or other dark colors are appropriate.

Attach the top of the batik with tacks or staples to the flat side of a piece of moulding. Put a piece of twill tape through each pot-holder ring and tack the ends to the moulding as in Illus. 34. Fasten a second piece of wood over the first with finishing nails and spot the nails with paint. Use the same method to finish the bottom with wood, but leave off the tape and rings. Now your batik is ready to be hung and admired!

HOW TO MAKE A FRAME

Materials
1 × 2-inch pine lumber
saw
hammer
chisel
ruler
pencil

Many people like to stretch the fabric on a frame, instead of laying it on a papered surface, while waxing a batik. The frame holds the cloth away from the work surface to prevent wax from sticking, and both sides of the cloth may be easily checked to see if the wax has penetrated properly. In addition, the design is easier to see this way than on cloth laid on waxed paper

Another use of a frame is to hold the cloth while painting on dye. If dye is brushed on a thin cloth laid on papers, it is apt to streak. With the cloth on the frame, the color can be brushed on more evenly.

You can buy an adjustable frame for batiks from art supply dealers or you can make one from four pieces of 1 × 2 inch pine lumber. The illustration shows a frame which can be

Illus. 35. An adjustable wooden frame is ideal for holding the cloth while you wax it.

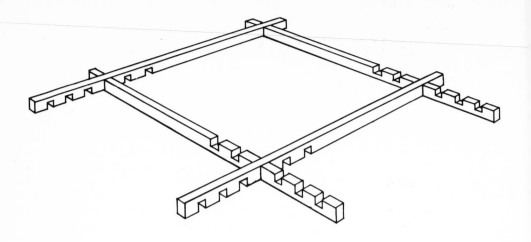

Illus. 36. Above is the way you would set up your frame for a large batik. The unslotted ends add length to the frame. Below (Illus. 37) is the way you would set up your frame for a small batik.

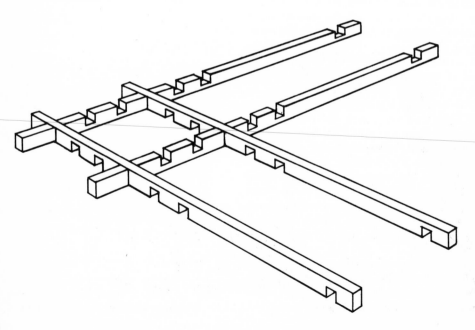

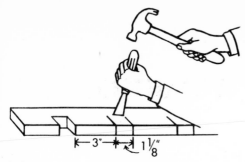

Illus. 38. After making parallel saw cuts, use a hammer and chisel to remove the wood for slots.

made as large as 45 by 45 inches, with interlocking slots 3 inches apart. The frame should not be larger than this because it is difficult to stretch large batiks so that they do not sag in the middle.

By cutting slots 3 inches apart along half of each piece of wood, with a single slot cut 3 inches from the opposite end, you can accommodate cloth of any size up to 6 inches less than the length of the wood pieces without needing to cut slots along the entire length of each piece. To arrange the frame for a small batik, you would use the slotted half of each piece and interlock the four pieces, ignoring the single end slots. To accommodate a larger batik, you would use the single end slots, with the plain half of each piece forming most of the frame and the slotted halves providing the additional length and width. (See Illus. 36 and 37.)

The slots are made by taking the 1-inch side of the lumber and sawing parallel cuts 1⅛ inches apart to exactly one half the depth of the 2-inch side of the lumber. Although called 2-inch lumber, the depth is slightly less. The wood is removed from the slot by placing a wood chisel between the inner ends of the cuts, then hitting the chisel with a hammer. The block of wood falls away, leaving a slot.

The frame can be made rigid by fastening a small furniture clamp diagonally in each corner. When working with it this way, the frame rests on the clamps, and the cloth is fastened to the opposite side.

To use the frame, fit the sides of the frame together so they are the same size as the edges of the cloth. Pin or tack small pieces of cloth by the corners only, stretching the cloth as smoothly as possible. You may need more tacks to keep larger pieces taut. Try to place the tacks along the same thread on each side to keep the cloth evenly stretched. Uneven stretching makes it difficult to draw straight lines, and curved lines will be uneven.

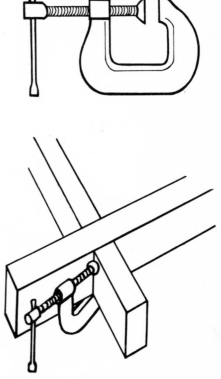

Illus. 39. Use a small furniture clamp (C clamp) to make the frame rigid.

HOW TO MAKE A TJANTING

Materials
    2 × 2-inch can
    brass tubing
    wooden handle
    No. 0 emery cloth
    hacksaw
    vise or clamp
    small tip 37½-watt electric soldering iron
    pliers
    small roll of rosin core solder
    ordinary straight pin
    tenpenny nail or an awl

A tjanting (pronounced chahn-ting) is a tool which is used to apply wax in fine lines or dots. This tool has been used for centuries in the Orient to make extremely complex batik designs for clothing. It consists of a handle, a reservoir to hold the wax, and a spout through which the wax flows.

Commercially-made tjantings are often available through art supply dealers. These are made from brass tubing, and hold a small amount of wax.

You can make a tjanting which holds a larger amount of wax, and which is easy to use. The wax reservoir is made from a small can of the type mushrooms are packed in. The spout is made from very fine brass tubing, available at hobby shops. Tubing of 1 to 2 mm. in diameter is suitable to use for the spout. The smaller diameter will make very fine lines, and the problem of stray drips

Illus. 40. A tool for drawing with wax is called a tjanting. At the top of this photo is a can tjanting made with a fine brass tubing spout and a wooden handle. Below is a tjanting made with an oil can spout; the wire handle is wrapped with rags. At the bottom is a commercial tjanting of brass.

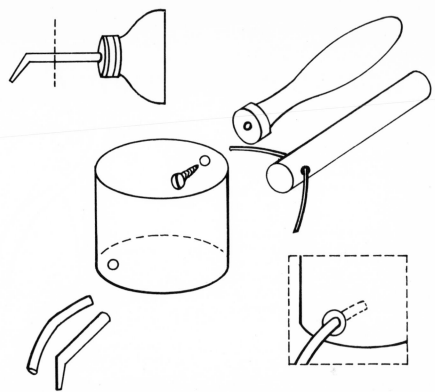

Illus. 41. Use an oil can spout (saw on the dotted line) or a piece of brass tubing inserted in a small can to make your own tjanting. The spout has to be soldered as shown in the diagram at the bottom right. Add wooden handle with a screw, or solder a dowel-and-wire handle to the sides of the can.

is easily controlled. The 2 mm. diameter tubing makes lines $\frac{1}{8}$ to $\frac{1}{4}$ inch wide, suitable for designs on a large scale. If you cannot get the brass tubing, the end of an oil can spout makes an acceptable substitute. (Cut the spout as shown in the diagram and proceed as with tubing.)

Place the tubing in a vise, or clamp it to a table to hold it firmly without squeezing. With the hacksaw, cut off a length $1\frac{1}{4}$ inches long, cutting slowly to keep the cut smooth. This small piece will become the spout.

Place the emery cloth on a firm surface, and

rub the cut end of the spout over the emery until the tube is smooth and free of rough edges. Remove any excess metal clogging the inside of the spout by pushing a straight pin in and out.

The spout has to be curved to make the tjanting work correctly. Don't bend the spout with the pliers directly, since this may cause a kink in the tubing and ruin the spout. Instead, bend the tubing around the neck of the wood handle as explained in the next paragraph.

Place the tubing at a right angle to the neck

of the wooden handle, and use the pliers to hold the tubing firmly against the handle. With your hand, bend the tubing slowly until a curve forms in the middle of the spout. You may need to move the tubing and reposition it as you bend. It should curve so that the end is bent downward at a 45° angle.

Using the tenpenny nail or an awl, punch a small hole in the side of the can just above the lower rim. Position this hole an inch or so away from the seam running down the side of the can. Try fitting the spout in the hole, and continue to enlarge the hole until the spout fits snugly through.

Clean the area on the front of the can around the spout hole with emery cloth, and also clean an area $\frac{1}{4}$ inch in length around the end of the spout to be soldered to the can. Insert a straight pin into the end of the spout to be soldered, pushing it in tight. The head of the pin will prevent solder from clogging the spout while you fasten the spout to the can.

Place the can on a flat surface, such as a table, allowing the spout to protrude over the edge. You may need to brace the spout with pliers to keep it from moving while you solder. Plug the soldering iron into an electric outlet. Hold the heated tip of the soldering iron against the can where it meets the top of the spout; then touch the end of the solder to the heated area. As it melts, flow

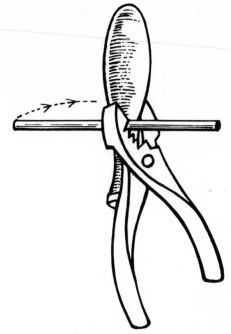

Illus. 42. Hold tubing in place with pliers and bend around wooden handle.

the solder around the spout, heating each area with the soldering iron as you go. Let the solder cool to harden. After the solder is hard, remove the pin from the spout.

Punch a hole in the *top* of the can opposite the spout, and fasten the handle with a screw.

HOW TO USE THE TJANTING

Whether you use a commercial tjanting or make your own, some practice is needed before you will be able to make smooth lines without blotches. You should practice on an extra piece of cloth until you can draw a quick, sure line.

Fill the tjanting by pouring wax into it, or by dipping it into the wax. The can tjanting should be no more than one-third full, the commercial tjanting no more than half full. If the tjanting is warm, wax may start dripping out the spout, so do not hold the tjanting over your batik until you are ready to wax.

To warm the wax to the correct temperature and to melt wax clogging the spout, place the bowl of the tjanting over the flame of an alcohol lamp. Lamps are available through laboratory or art supply dealers. The lamps burn denatured alcohol, which you can buy at a drugstore.

As you hold the tjanting over the flame, you will see the wax moving in waves or lines across the bottom of the can. Now pass the spout briefly through the flame until wax starts to drip out. If the wax is too hot, it will run out of the spout or drip very rapidly. The wax will drip slowly and steadily if the temperature is about right.

Test the temperature by making a line or dot on extra cloth. If the wax spreads a great deal, it is too hot. If the wax builds up on the cloth without flattening and going into the fibres, it is too cold.

Hold a small rag under the spout to keep the wax from running out, and move the tjanting to the batik. Remove the rag when you are ready to draw, and quickly move the tjanting along the lines of the design, with the spout barely touching the cloth. After the line is completed, place the rag under the spout to prevent drips on the cloth.

Keep the wax at the correct temperature while you work by periodically reheating the tjanting over the alcohol lamp. Be careful not to get the rag close to the flame while you are reheating the tjanting, or it may catch on fire.

When you are finished using the tjanting, pour the wax remaining in the reservoir back into the pot of wax. The next time you use the tjanting, the thin layer of wax covering the interior of the reservoir will melt quickly when new wax is poured into it.

A commercial tjanting is used in the same way as the can tjanting, but since it is smaller, you will have to refill the reservoir more often.

Illus. 43. Warm the wax by placing the wax reservoir over the flame of an alcohol lamp.

Illus. 44. Hold a rag under the spout to keep the wax from running out as you move the tjanting over the batik.

Illus. 45. Remove the rag from under the spout and quickly draw the wax line. Replace the rag under the spout when you are finished drawing the line.

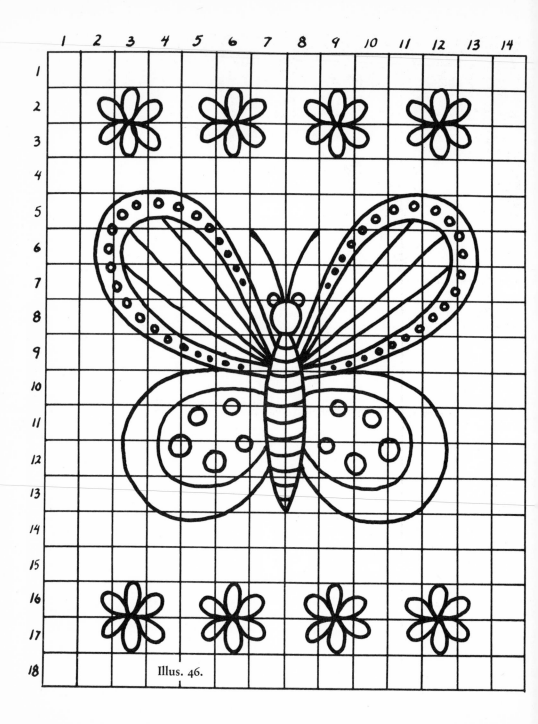

Illus. 46.

PROJECT FOUR: A TJANTING DESIGN WALL HANGING

Materials
  14 × 18 inch fine, white cotton
  tjanting
  alcohol lamp
  three colors of dye
  newspapers and waxed paper, or frame
  small brush

Your first project with the tjanting will be small in order to make waxing easier. It also has a confetti-like background of dots to hide any accidental drips. You may add your own embellishments to the design at each stage in the waxing, if you wish to make a fancier butterfly, than the one illustrated here and on color page D.

Yellow, red, and blue dyes were used to make the illustrated batik. A combination of yellow, blue and brown would also work well. Mix the dyes according to the directions given for household dyes in Project One, or according to manufacturer's directions for batik dyes.

Enlarge and transfer your design; then stretch the cloth on a frame or lay it flat on papers. Using the tjanting, outline the butterfly and flowers with wax. The flower petals may be drawn free-hand and do not have to be perfectly symmetrical. Make the wax spots on the butterfly's wings. Allow the tjanting to drip freely, and move it over the background, holding it above the surface of the cloth, to make dots. Everything waxed now will remain white.

Illus. 47. Wax the outlines and drip wax on the background. It is ready to be dyed yellow.

Illus. 48. Wax the flower petals and the edges of the wings. Drip wax over the background. The batik is ready to be dyed red.

Dye the batik in the lightest color, yellow. Rinse and dry.

After the batik is dry, use a small brush dipped in wax to fill in the areas which will remain yellow—the flowers and the edges of the butterfly's wings. If you can feel the roughness of the cloth through the wax, the wax is too thin and needs to be recoated. Try letting the wax cool a little before doing any more waxing with the brush, as hot wax tends to sink through the cloth, leaving the rough surface which will stain with the next dyeing.

Use the tjanting to drip wax over the background and to draw a line down each side of the butterfly's body next to the white outline. You may add extra lines and spots on the butterfly, if you wish. These also will remain yellow.

Dye the batik red. Rinse and dry. Areas which were dyed yellow and not waxed will now be orange.

Use the brush to fill in the butterfly's head and body, and the central area of the wings, with wax. Drip wax over the background with the tjanting. The waxed areas will remain orange. Dye the darkest color, blue. Because of the combination of the three colors, the background will not be blue but a brownish grey.

After the batik is dry, brush a light coat of wax on the background so the entire batik is covered with wax, then iron all the wax out. Since this is a wall hanging, it is not necessary to dry-clean it, and the wax will enhance the color.

Trim the sides of the batik, or turn the edges over and hem them. Frame the top and bottom edges.

Illus. 49. Wax the interior of the wings and the body and drip more wax in empty spaces on the background. It is ready to be dyed blue.

MIXING COLORS IN DYEING

All colors may be created by mixing the three primary colors, red, yellow, and blue. Since dyes are available premixed to almost any color, it is usually simpler to buy the colors you want rather than to try to create them yourself.

However, you still need to know something about mixing colors, because dyeing one color over another causes the colors to mix on the cloth and become a third color. The chart on the next page will give you an idea of the resulting color when one color is dyed over another.

Use the chart as a guide to help plan dyeing sequences. By dyeing from the lightest color to the darkest, you should be able to use a few dyes to create several colors.

Tints of a color are formed by adding more water to the dye, or by immersing the fabric in the dye bath for a very short time. If you dye a dark color over a light color, and leave the batik in the dark dye bath a long time, the light color will be covered up. Rather than getting a blend of the two colors, such as red and yellow to make orange, only the darker color, red, will show. Mixing colors thus depends partly on the length of time the batik is in the dye bath.

Every project in this book except the last one uses a sequence of dyeing in which wax covers one color after another without being removed until the end. This is a simple way to make a batik and it allows you to have a freedom of choice with a number of colors. Using this method, a dyeing sequence starting with yellow could proceed either from yellow to orange to red to brown, or from yellow to green to blue-green to brown, but you cannot change from orange to green. As the chart shows, green over orange will produce a light greenish-brown. Blue, which you would use over yellow to produce green, will produce brown if used over orange. So you must remove the wax over the original yellow by means of solvents, and redye the cloth blue to get green.

It is therefore simpler to paint on dyes when you want many colors. By painting, you can confine the dye to one spot rather than covering the entire batik as you do with dip dyeing. In addition, repeated dyeing of an area tends to dull the color, and for this reason also, painting dye is better when you are using a large number of colors.

Dye your batiks in the way that will be easiest for you. Both dipping and painting are used in this book, and both methods give good results.

	over yellow produces	over red produces	over blue produces	over orange produces	over green produces	over purple produces	over brown produces
yellow	deep yellow	orange	green	light orange	light green	reddish brown	yellowish brown
red	orange	deep red	purple	dark red-orange	brown	wine red	dark reddish brown
blue	green	purple	deep blue	brown	blue-green	bluish purple	very dark brown
orange	light orange	dark red-orange	brown	deep orange	light greenish brown	reddish brown	golden brown
green	light green	brown	blue-green	light greenish brown	dark green	dull purplish grey	olive green
purple	reddish brown	wine red	bluish purple	reddish brown	dull purplish grey	deep purple	dark reddish brown
brown	yellowish brown	dark reddish brown	dark grey	golden brown	dull greenish brown	dark reddish brown	dark brown

Illus. 50. This chart tells you what result to expect when you dye one color over another. Use it as a guide to plan your sequence of dyeing. Always remember to start with the lightest color.

MAKING CRACKLE LINES

Crackle lines often enhance a batik design by giving an interesting texture to otherwise plain areas. It is used as an important part of the design in some of the remaining projects. By following a few simple steps, you should be able to get good crackle with sharp lines that will make your batiks more interesting.

After it is washed, the cloth should be starched to get the best crackle. Starching the cloth makes the color of the webbing brighter and the lines crisper than they would be on unstarched cloth. When liquid laundry starch is used, mixtures ranging from two to six parts water to one part starch are satisfactory, depending on the thickness of the cloth. For a fabric such as cotton broadcloth, a four-part water to one-part starch mixture is good. Iron the starched cloth and wax it as you normally would.

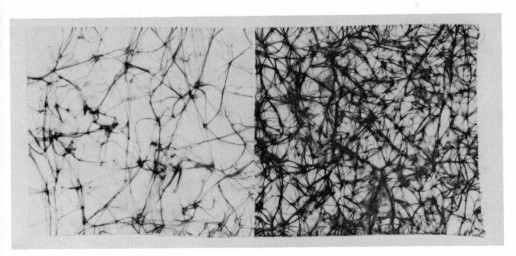

Illus. 51. The crackle at the left was made by lightly crushing the waxed cloth. Heavy crushing of the cloth on the right resulted in many more lines. Both samples were dyed overnight.

For crackle, the wax mixture should be at least 75 per cent hard paraffin, which is more brittle than beeswax. It is even better to use pure paraffin to wax the cloth for crackling, even if you use a mixture to wax your design. To *avoid* crackle, pure beeswax is used, although it too will crack if the waxed cloth is creased or folded sharply.

You can apply wax to the cloth for crackling either by painting it on or by dipping the cloth into the wax. If you dip the cloth into the wax, the wax (paraffin) should be no more than 5 to 10 degrees above its melting point (131 degrees F. to 140 degrees F., or 55 degrees C. to 60 degrees C.). The easiest way to obtain the right temperature is to pour melted wax into a large pan, and let it cool until a skin begins to form across the top; then check the temperature with a thermometer made to be immersed in liquids. Laboratory immersion thermometers or candy thermometers are suitable.

Stir to dissolve the skin, then dip in the cloth, making sure it is completely covered with wax. Pull the cloth out with tongs and let it drain, turning the cloth to keep the wax coating even. Hold the cloth in the air until the surface is dry; then it may be laid on newspapers to cool.

It is very difficult to control the temperature of the wax if, instead of dipping the cloth, you are painting the wax on, because the wax cools rapidly on the brush. However, this is often the only way you can make the design. If you paint the wax on to be crackled, it must be at least 170 degrees F. or 76 degrees C. in order to penetrate the cloth. The wax can be hotter. The coating must be thick. Paint both sides of the cloth with wax a *second* time, after the first layer has cooled, to be sure that the cloth is well covered with wax. The wax coating should feel smooth; any rough spots indicate a thin coating of wax.

After the wax coating has cooled, chill the cloth with cold, running water up to 60 degrees F., or dip it briefly in ice water to harden the wax. Crush the cloth, bending it back and forth with your hands. Heavy crushing makes many crackle lines; lighter crushing, fewer lines. After crushing lightly and straightening out the cloth, hold it to the light to get an idea of the number of lines. If you want more, crush it again.

If you want only certain areas to have crackle, reseal the wax where no crackle is desired by repainting the area with wax, or by touching it with the tip of a warm iron to melt the wax.

After straightening, the crushed cloth is ready for the dye bath. Soak the waxed cloth several hours or overnight in dye, to be sure of complete color saturation. Don't paint the dye on for crackle, because it won't penetrate the cracks well. Since the wax-covered cloth tends to float, you may need to weight it with some heavy, glass objects such as ashtrays. The dye bath should cover the cloth completely.

After the dyeing is finished, rinse the batik until the surface is free of all dye spots; then let it dry thoroughly. You may be tempted to iron the wax out right away. Don't do it. The dye lines will run, making fuzzy, blotchy lines instead of a crisp network of veins.

This batiked corduroy wall hanging is called "Partridge in a Pear Tree." Explicit directions for waxing the cloth and painting on the dyes are given in Project Three.

With different waxing and dyeing, the same pattern, the sun design from Project Six, can result in a variety of batiks used to make pillows. Here are two variations that harmonize with each other.

A stylized cat with three large flowers make up this wall hanging. Note the crackled background and the stripes scratched on the cat. For complete instructions see Project Seven.

B

Decorated place mats dress up a table setting. These simple batiks are your first project.

Two examples of brush designs illustrate the diversity you can obtain even when using the same techniques. (Project Two.)

C

Where the design must be carefully drawn in wax, as in this wall hanging (Project Four), you use a special tool called a "tjanting."

This elaborate lampshade was created from drawing paper and batiked fabric. The cloth has two geometric borders and is heavily crackled. You will find border patterns and directions for constructing the shade in Project Five.

D

You can repeat your design as many as four times without redrawing it, merely by folding the cloth. The cotton voile scarf above was folded in half twice. The unicorn wall hanging below has a repeat border made by folding the organdy cloth in half.

E

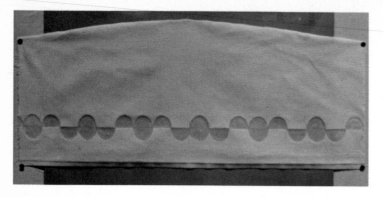

This is the first step in making the hood shown on the opposite page. The waxed white cloth is ready to be dyed yellow.

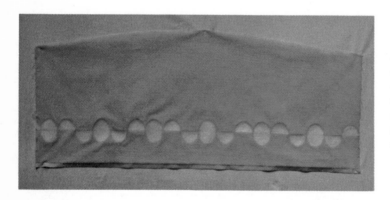

After the yellow dyeing, the wax must be completely removed with solvent before the cloth is waxed again to make a multicolor design.

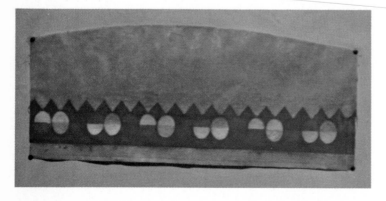

Here is the batik after being dyed red. Now it should show four colors—white, yellow, orange and red. The wax is again removed with solvent and the cloth is rewaxed.

F

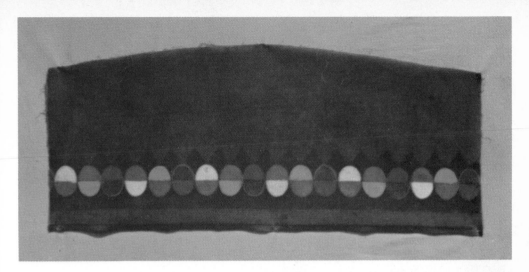

The blue dyeing results in eight colors—white, yellow, orange, red, blue, green, purple and brown. The same three primary colors and the same sequence in dyeing can result in either a red or a green hood depending upon the waxing pattern you choose. (See Project Nine.) This hood was done in velveteen.

The pattern for this repeat design scarf and the dyeing instructions are detailed in Project Eight.

A variation of Project Seven is this cat design wall hanging which makes use of dark outlines to set off the main motif from the background.

PROJECT FIVE: A BATIK LAMPSHADE

Materials
- newspapers
- masking tape
- large sheets of white drawing paper
- pencil
- yardstick or ruler
- scissors
- razor blade
- white glue
- old lampshade
- bleached (white) or light, unbleached muslin
- tjanting or brush
- small brush for dye
- alcohol lamp
- dyes—household or batik
- large pans
- waxed paper or frame
- liquid laundry starch

You can convert an old lampshade into a beautiful glowing jewel that will enhance almost any type of décor. Batik is especially striking with light shining through it, and crackle can be used to add a marble-like texture to the shade. Any number of colors can be used by painting the dyes on.

The shade is made by making a new covering of drawing paper fastened to the hoops of the old shade. The drawing-paper base is covered with the batiked cloth.

The illustrated shade (see color page D), which is large, consists of a 2-inch and a 4-inch border with a crackled middle. The borders should be proportionate to the size of your shade, therefore several designs are shown in the diagrams.

In order to tell how much cloth to use, you must first make a pattern the size of the shade. Fasten newspapers tightly around the old lampshade, covering it completely and using masking tape to fasten the sheets to each other. Do not fasten them to the shade. Trim the excess paper from the top and bottom edges of the shade, and remove the paper by making one cut from top to bottom. The paper will be your pattern for cutting the cloth to the shape of the lampshade.

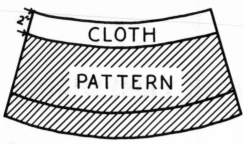

Illus. 52. Get the proper curve for the border by sliding the newspaper pattern down on the cloth.

Wash the cloth to preshrink it; then iron it. Lay the newspaper pattern on the cloth and pin it in place. Cut out the shape, allowing a 1-inch margin all around the edges of the pattern. The extra margins at the top and bottom will be used to fasten the lampshade over the wire hoops. The other margins will be used for a vertical seam. Save the paper pattern as you will need it again, for the batik and to make the drawing-paper frame.

To draw a top border, mark off the height of the border at two sides on the end of the cloth. Lay the paper pattern on the cloth, lining up the sides of the pattern and cloth. Slide the pattern down until the top edge touches the marks. The top edge of the pattern should parallel the edge of the cloth, making it easy to draw a curved line along the border, as shown in the diagram. For a bottom border, follow the same procedure, sliding the pattern up instead of down. The bottom edge of the pattern will be parallel to the bottom edge of the cloth, allowing you to draw that curve correctly. Pencil it in.

Each pattern suggested here shows a portion of the border design, which is to be repeated over and over again around the border. As a general rule, make the top border half the size of the lower border. Three pairs of borders are shown, with designs for both the top and bottom borders to be used on a shade.

You can pencil in the design elements of the borders free-hand, or you can draw a small section on paper and trace it over and over again, by moving the diagram along under the cloth. To save time drawing, you may pencil in just the main design elements and wax the remainder free-hand.

If you are making a large shade, the work will go much faster if you use the large-spouted tjanting to draw many of the details free-hand, as well as to draw pencilled-in elements. Be sure to test the tjanting first on a scrap of cloth to see how much control you will have over the design. If it results in details that are too large, use the fine tjanting or a small brush.

Paint dyes on with a brush on *dry* cloth. Not wetting the cloth prevents the dye from running into unwanted areas. Wax and color each area as indicated in the diagrams showing various borders. As usual, work from the lightest color to the darkest. Show off light-colored dots by leaving an unwaxed area around each dot. Paint the area black or brown for contrast.

Illus. 53. Pattern for a 1-inch border. Step 1 (left): Wax triangle outlines and the top and bottom of border on white cloth, then paint the border with gold dye. Step 2 (middle): Wax oval shapes, then paint green. Step 3 (right): Wax a dot in the middle of each triangle, then paint brown. Use brown crackle on the remainder of the shade. (See Illus. 57 for paired border.)

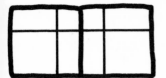 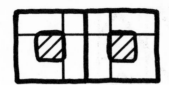 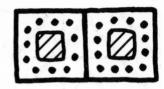

Illus. 54. Pattern for 1½-inch border. Step 1 (left): Wax the outlines of the squares, then paint the squares green. Step 2 (middle): Wax a small square in the middle of each large square. Paint the remainder blue, to get blue-green. Step 3 (right): Dot the blue-green edge with wax, then dye brown or black. Use blue, black or brown crackle on rest of shade.

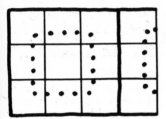 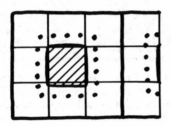 

Illus. 55. Pattern for a 3-inch border. Step 1 (left): Wax outlines of squares and make dots as shown. Paint with green dye. Step 2 (middle): Wax a solid square as shown and paint on blue dye, giving blue-green. Step 3 (right): Draw a line outside the white dots and make large dots of wax between the two outer wax lines. Paint the unwaxed areas brown or black.

Illus. 56. Pattern for a 2-inch border. Step 1 (left): Wax edges of border, triangles and dots. Paint triangles green and middle of border yellow. Step 2 (middle): Wax ovals and areas of triangles shown by shaded lines. Paint middle of border red. Step 3 (right): Wax dots as shown, then paint entire border brown. Crackle shade with blue or brown. This border pairs with the one in Illus. 58.

After you have completed the waxing and dyeing, rinse the excess dye out. Use a large vessel if possible, to keep the cloth from folding over on itself and staining the unwaxed areas. If areas are stained, or the dye runs, the crackle design will cover much of it, so don't worry too much about it. After the cloth is rinsed and dried, dip it in a solution of four parts water to one part liquid laundry starch and let it dry again.

Illus. 57. Pattern for a 2-inch border. Step 1 (top): Wax triangle outlines and top and bottom of border, then paint the border with gold dye. Step 2 (left): Wax shaded areas shown. Paint the border green. Step 3 (right): Wax a dot in each upper triangle; paint upper triangles brown. Wax shaded diagonal bands. Paint the band with the oval shapes brown, and leave the lower small triangles green so that the border has alternating bands of color.

Illus. 58. Pattern for a 4-inch border. Step 1 (left): Wax oval lines and dots. Paint each entire oval yellow. Alternate green and blue triangles outside ovals. Step 2 (middle): Wax another row of dots, a smaller oval within each large one, and a wavy line as shown. Leave triangles and dotted areas undyed. Paint the rest red. Step 3 (right): Wax a row of dots around middle oval and wax shaded areas of wavy lines as shown. Wax small triangles within larger ones. Paint entire border with brown dye.

To make the crackle, pour melted paraffin wax into a large pan and let it cool. Spread newspapers on the floor and set the pan of wax on the papers. Dip the batik into the pan, covering the cloth completely with wax; then hold it in the air until the surface is dry. As soon as it is dry to the touch, the cloth may be laid on papers to cool.

Allow the cloth to cool thoroughly before attempting to chill it, otherwise the crackle

Illus. 59. To dye one section at a time, hold it under the dye with a glass weight. After the crackle appears, move the batik and dye the next section.

will not turn out well. Chill the batik in cold water, crush, then straighten it out.

If you have a large vessel, you can immerse the entire batik in dark-colored dye, or dye one section at a time. To dye a section at a time, start at one end and immerse a section in the dye, holding the section under the dye with a glass weight. After 30 minutes, check the appearance. If the crackle lines are satisfactory, move the cloth until a new section is in the dye, and the edge of the previously dyed section just touches the surface of the dye bath. Leave each section in the dye as long as necessary to obtain clear crackle lines. After the dyeing is completed, rinse the batik thoroughly and hang it to dry.

After it is dry, iron the wax out, using many changes of paper to absorb the heavy layer of wax. When the paper will not absorb any more wax, the batik is finished except for shaping. No more wax is removed after ironing, as the wax makes the batik shade more translucent.

After ironing, lay the batik on the news-paper pattern. If the batik is stretched out of shape, iron one area at a time and stretch it into shape again while the cloth is hot; then iron it smooth.

With the batik done, you are ready to construct the shade. Lay several sheets of white drawing paper next to each other in a line, and place the newspaper pattern on top. The number of sheets of drawing paper the pattern partially or completely covers is the amount you will need to cut to make the shade.

For the shade illustrated in this book three and one-half sheets of drawing paper were covered by the pattern. Rather than have uneven sections, the pattern was folded into fourths, and four even sections were cut. Depending on the size of your shade, you may need from two to four sections of drawing paper.

Fold your own newspaper pattern in half, in thirds, or in fourths as needed to provide equal sections. Cut one section along the folds to use as a pattern for cutting the

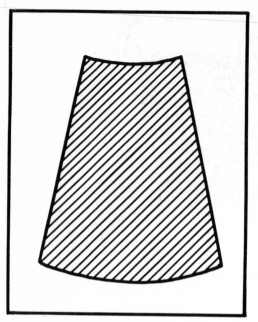

drawing paper to shape. Lay the small newspaper section on a sheet of drawing paper and trace around it. Trace as many sections as you need. Use the yardstick or ruler to draw a $\frac{1}{4}$-inch margin on the left side of each section. Also add a $\frac{1}{2}$-inch margin to the top and bottom of each section.

Cut the sections out, and make tabs on the top and bottom margins by clipping the margin every inch. Save a tab every 3 or 4 inches, and cut the rest away.

Lay some waxed paper on a table or the floor, and lay the drawing-paper sections on the waxed paper. Coat the $\frac{1}{4}$-inch margin on the side of all the sections but the outermost with white glue, and glue the sections together. You should now have a flat shape of drawing paper the same size as the original lampshade pattern, made of sections with $\frac{1}{4}$-inch seams. Let the glue dry thoroughly, so the sections won't come apart as you work with the shade.

Illus. 60. Fold the newspaper pattern into even sections. Cut out and use one section (shaded shape) as a pattern to cut the drawing paper.

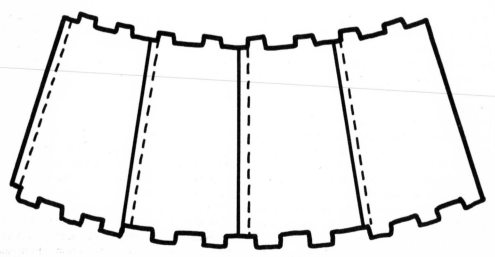

Illus. 61. Drawing paper sections glued together to form shade has tabs for fastening.

Use a knife or razor blade to cut the hoops out of the old lampshade. Remove all the material from the hoops until you have only the bare wire.

Bend the drawing paper until it forms a cylinder, and use masking tape to hold the vertical seam together. Bend all the tabs, top and bottom, inward toward the middle of the cylinder. Set the cylinder on end and drop in the bottom wire hoop. Tape the hoop in place by bending the tabs over it, and holding the tabs down with masking tape. Fasten the top hoop the same way.

By taping the shade together, you have a more rigid shape to work with, and gluing is easier than if you tried to glue the flat drawing paper directly around a hoop.

Start gluing by working from the middle of the drawing paper shape to the outer edges (the one remaining unglued seam). Remove the tape from a few tabs and dot them with glue. Line up the edge of the paper and the hoop; then fasten the tabs tightly over the hoop. Be sure the paper is stretched tightly around the hoop as you glue. Work first toward one end, then the other, but don't glue down the tabs which are right next to the seam. Wait until you have finished gluing the second hoop. Glue the second hoop the same way.

The one remaining vertical seam may be slightly uneven after you have finished gluing the hoops. Trim, or add a narrow strip of paper if necessary, and glue the seam. Glue the remaining tabs at the top and bottom.

Tape the batik around the paper shade with masking tape, and adjust it until the edges of the margins line up with the wire hoops. The batik should fit smoothly over the paper and should look even.

Trim the excess margin of cloth from the top and the bottom until a $\frac{3}{8}$-inch margin of cloth remains. Put white glue on the inside

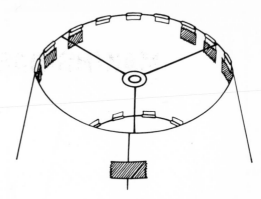

Illus. 62. Glue the tabs over the hoop by removing the tape from a few tabs at a time. Stretch the paper shade smoothly around the hoop.

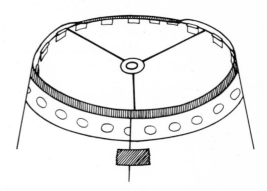

Illus. 63. Place glue on the inside of the wire hoop and stretch the batiked cloth over it.

of the wire hoop (no glue on the outside of the lampshade), and stretch the cloth margin over the wire, working from the middle to the ends. Complete both hoops.

Trim the margins of the vertical seam until there is a $\frac{1}{4}$-inch overlap. Glue the seam. Now your shade is ready to be placed on the lamp. Turn on the light to see the beautiful effect of the translucent batik.

55

MAKING DARK OUTLINES

Illus. 64. The bird at the top left was drawn with a tjanting and the cloth was dyed, resulting in a light line on a dark background (top right). Everything except the outline of the bird was waxed on the cloth at the bottom left, resulting in a dark outline after dyeing (bottom right).

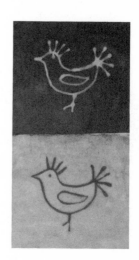

The natural way to draw with the tjanting is to use it like a pencil, outlining the design with wax. After the cloth is dyed, the wax line is lighter than the background. There are times when you might prefer a dark outline around an object. This takes a little more planning, but should not be difficult once you understand the principle.

The illustration shows a bird made with a dark outline and a bird with a light outline. The light line was drawn directly with the tjanting, then dyed. The tjanting was also used to form an outline for the second bird, but the background and interior of the bird were filled in with wax, leaving an unwaxed channel which became a dark outline after the cloth was dyed.

Since the entire cloth must be covered with wax to make a dark outline, the outline has to be the last step if you are going to use more than one color. You have to remember to leave an unwaxed channel around each object as you cover succeeding colors with wax. The next two projects use several colors and have dark outlines to set off the designs

PROJECT SIX: SUN DESIGN PILLOW

Materials

two 16 × 16-inch unbleached muslin
    squares
brown and yellow dye—household or
    batik
fine-spouted tjanting
alcohol lamp
newspapers and waxed paper, or frame
brush
dry-cleaning solvent (optional)
pillow stuffing

Illus. 65. After tracing the design, tack cloth on frame and outline with tjanting.

Illus. 66. Pattern for sun design pillow.

The sun design pillow can be made several ways for interesting variety—round or square, with a white or with a yellow background. (See color page B.) The yellow background, square pillow is discussed in detail first, with instructions for the other pillows given at the end of the chapter.

You will need a steady hand to wax the straight edges of the sun rays, but as with all batiks, you should not try for mechanical perfection. By using the fine-spouted 1-mm. tjanting, you can wax a fine line without having to move your hand too quickly, and you should be able to follow the lines.

Illus. 67. Wax the whites of the eyes, half the face, and half of each ray. Dye the white cloth yellow.

Starch and iron the cloth; then trace the design. You can transfer the ray design more easily if you cut out a piece of paper the size of the ray and trace around it. The base is 2 inches wide; the height of the triangle is 2¾ inches.

Waxing is easier if you outline the areas first; then fill them in with the tjanting or brush. Place the tjanting in the middle of the area you plan to wax; then move the spout over to the edge and wax around the line. This way you won't have blots or drips on the outline.

If you make a mistake, scrape the wax off carefully with a knife, and use a cotton swab dipped in spot remover or dry cleaning solvent to blot up any wax left in the cloth after scraping. Try not to make mistakes, as these spots often won't dye as well as the rest of the cloth.

Cover one half of each ray, the whites of both eyes, and half the face with wax. Leave the broad line that defines the nose, mouth, and outside of the face unwaxed throughout *all* the steps of waxing and dyeing. Follow the diagrams closely. Also leave the middle and the exterior outline of the eye unwaxed. All of these unwaxed lines will be dyed brown in the last dyeing, to form the outlines.

After the first waxing, dye the cloth yellow, and save the dye. When the batik is dry, cover the yellow background with hot wax, leaving the yellow portion of the sun and of the rays unwaxed. After the wax layer cools, go over it again so the surface feels smooth, because the background will be crackled later.

Make gold dye by adding a small quantity of brown to the yellow dye bath, or use premixed gold dye. You can test your home-

Illus. 68. Cover the yellow background with wax, leaving half the face and the remaining halves of the rays unwaxed. Dye gold.

made gold on a wet scrap of cloth. If the cloth is yellow, not gold, add more brown and test again until the color is to your satisfaction. Rewarm the dye by heating a portion of it in a pot on the stove; then mix the hot and cold dye together. Dye the batik gold. After it is dry, wax the remaining half

of the face, leaving the outline unwaxed as shown in the last diagram. Check to see if there are any thin or peeling spots of wax on the rest of the batik, and rewax these if necessary.

Chill the cloth with cold water and crush the batik. Straighten it out and put it in a

Illus. 69. Wax the remaining half of the face and dye brown.

brown dye bath, so it is completely covered with dye. Leave it in the dye from at least 1 hour to overnight. Rinse and dry the batik; then iron the wax out.

It is nice to dry-clean the batik, before making it into a pillow, to give it a softer surface. Use a non-flammable solvent if possible, as suggested in Project One. Use a glass or stainless steel bowl, and dip the batik in the solvent until the cloth is soft.

After it is dry and the solvent smell is gone, iron the batik with spray sizing or starch to give it a finish, and make it into a pillow following the directions in Project Two.

Round pillows can be made by drawing the design on 16-inch circles of muslin, rather than on squares.

To make a yellow sun on a white background, wax and dye in the following steps:

1. Wax the whites of the eyes, and the background, leaving all the rays and sun unwaxed.

2. Dye yellow.

3 Wax half the face, and half of each ray.

4. Dye gold.

5. Cover the remaining half of the face and rays with wax.

6. Chill the cloth, crush, and dye brown.

Illus. 70. Pattern for a cat and flower design. Each double outline represents a ¼-inch channel that remains unwaxed throughout all the dyeings.

PROJECT SEVEN: CAT DESIGN WALL HANGING

Materials
16 × 25-inch cotton cloth
tjanting
alcohol lamp
brush
yellow, red, green and brown dye—
   household or batik
newspapers and waxed paper, or frame
stylus, nut pick, or knitting needle

A perky cat design can be made in two versions, the simpler with a brush only, and the more complicated with both a tjanting and brush. The cat with flowers is described first.

Starch and iron the cloth before waxing. Wax each section of the cat's body by outlining with the fine-spouted tjanting, then fill in the areas solidly with wax (see Step 1), using the tjanting or brush. The fine lines on

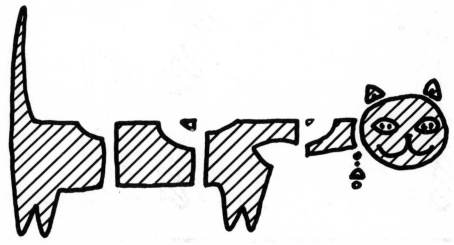

Illus. 71. Step 1: First wax only the cat's body. Follow the pattern closely. Remain inside the double outline.

Illus. 72. Step 2: Wax the head. Leave un-waxed channels for eyes, nose, and mouth.

the cat will be added last by scratching them in. Wax the cat's head as shown in Step 2.

Dye the batik yellow. Rinse the batik and let it dry. Dot the middle of the central flower with wax, using the tjanting. Wax the background of the batik, following the diagram in Step 3, leaving space for the flowers, stems, and leaves. In addition, leave approximately a ¼-inch channel all around the cat. (See pattern.) The channel will become the outline later.

After the cloth is dry, paint red dye on the yellow flowers until they turn orange. Do not wet the cloth before dyeing. Painting the dye on dry cloth helps keep it from running. Since this is a small area, any streaking caused by the dry cloth won't show. Rinse the batik and let it dry.

Illus. 73. Step 3: After the batik is dyed yellow, wax the background and dot the central flower. (Grey area is white body of the cat.)

Illus. 74. Wax orange flower petals and dots. Paint red dye on outer flowers and green dye on the grass and leaves.

Wax the petals of the flowers, staying about ¼ inch away from the waxed background and leaving a circle in the middle of each flower. The flower petals will remain orange. Next, wax the orange dots in the circles of the outer flowers; then paint the rest of the area in the circles with red dye until they turn red. The circle in the middle flower will be dyed brown in the last dyeing.

Wet the cloth, and paint green dye on the stems, leaves, and grass areas. Rinse the batik and let it dry.

Use the tjanting to draw a stem for each flower, leaving unwaxed cloth on either side of the covered green stem. Wax the green leaves and grass, leaving a ¼-inch channel around each. Cover the middle parts of the outer flowers with wax, leaving a narrow channel outlining the space between the circle and petals. This completes the waxing, except for any needed retouching.

Feel the batik to see if the wax is thick enough. Any rough spots indicate thin areas. Since the yellow background will be

Illus. 75. Wax the stem with a line from the tjanting. Leave unwaxed channels around the stem and the leaves.

crackled, if the wax coating seems thin, you should rewax the entire front and back of the batik, except for the parts to be dyed brown. The design will show clearly on the back because the wax will have penetrated the cloth.

After waxing is complete, use the stylus, nut pick, or knitting needle to scratch

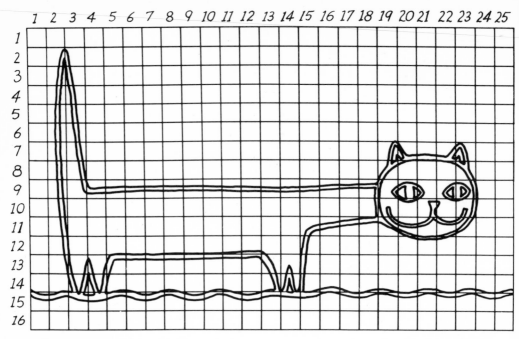

<figure> Illus. 76. Pattern for a plain cat design. Double outline indicates unwaxed channels. </figure>

stripes and whiskers on the cat. The object used should be pointed but not sharp enough to tear the cloth. Scratch the front surface only.

After the stripes and whiskers are drawn, chill the batik with cold water, then crush it. Dip the batik in dark brown dye until the crackle lines show. The brown dye will also dye all the unwaxed channels around the cat and flowers, forming dark outlines. After rinsing and drying the cloth, iron the wax out and frame the batik.

As a variation, a version of the cat may be done entirely with a brush, if you wish. Blue, green and brown dyes were used for the one in this book. (See color page H.) Wax the cat by using a brush or tjanting to draw the shape; then fill in the body and head with

wax, leaving channels on the face as before. Dip in the blue dye.

After the dye has been rinsed and dried, repair any cracked places on the cat; then wax the background, staying about ¼ inch away from the cat, to form the outline all around.

Dip or paint on green for the grass. Next, wax the grass, leaving a ¼-inch channel unwaxed between the grass and the background.

Scratch lines on the cat and draw whiskers with the stylus or knitting needle; then chill the cloth and crush it. Dip in brown dye until crackle is formed. After the cloth is rinsed and dried, iron the wax out and frame the batik.

PROJECT EIGHT: REPEAT DESIGN SCARF

Materials
   36 × 36-inch square of nylon chiffon
   two colors of silk dye
   glacial acetic acid
      or
   36 × 36-inch square of cotton voile
   two colors of cotton dye

   felt pen
   waxed paper
   drawing board or large cardboard
   tjanting
   alcohol lamp
   straight pins or thumbtacks
   small brush
   dry-cleaning solvent

Repeat designs can cover the entire batik or can be confined to only the border of the cloth. First we will consider covering the entire cloth.

The scarf design which you will make is created by folding the cloth into four layers, then waxing while the cloth is still folded. After the cloth is dyed and the wax is ironed out, it is a pleasant surprise to open the folds and find the design repeated four times. This type of design is most effective when part of the design touches the fold. After the cloth is opened, each section of the design is a mirror image of the other. (See color pages E and H.)

The cloth may be folded into fourths diagonally, lengthwise, or once in half, then in half again to make a smaller square. The last-mentioned method of folding is used to make the scarf pattern in this chapter. Don't fold the material into more than four layers because the wax won't penetrate any further layers.

Nylon, which makes a soft scarf material, must be dyed with special dyes to get true color values. If you are unable to obtain silk dyes, you may substitute cotton voile for the nylon and use cotton dyes.

Wash and press the cloth. Fold in half and press the fold, then fold in half again to

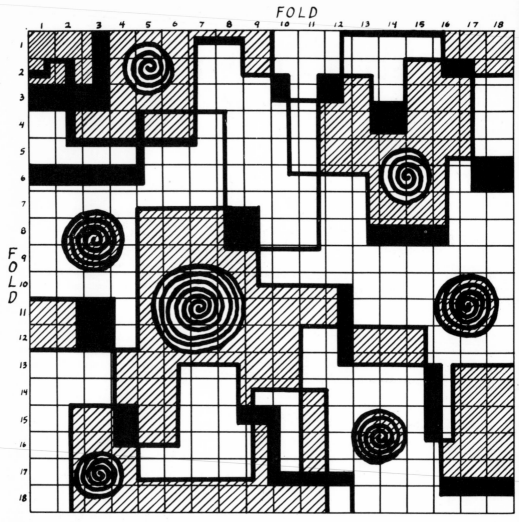

Illus. 77. The pattern for a repeat design scarf. The material is folded and the edges of the pattern are placed on the folds so that the design is repeated four times. (See finished scarf on color page H.)

make four layers, and press. Pin the edges together if necessary to keep the cloth from slipping as you press.

Make an enlarged pattern from the one in this book. Go over the enlarged pattern with a broad-tipped felt pen, making the lines heavy and marking in the solid areas, which are to be waxed on the first waxing. At this point, you need not concern yourself with the shaded areas indicated on the pattern in the book.

Lay your pattern on a smooth board or thick cardboard and cover it with waxed paper. Lay the folded cloth over the pattern, and place pins or tacks around the edges to stretch the cloth smooth and flat. The folds should be placed on the sides of the pattern marked "fold." You should be able to see the pattern underneath the cloth, making it unnecessary to transfer the design.

The large-spouted tjanting is well-suited to this project, because of the thickness of the layers of cloth.

Follow the pattern underneath, and trace the outlines on the cloth with the wax-filled tjanting; then fill in the solid areas.

If the cloth is not flat, or if the wax is too hot, the top layer may not have much wax on it. If spots appear to be thin, carefully rewax them. It is better not to rewax narrow lines if you can avoid doing so, as the wax often runs off the line and makes blobs. On the other hand, if the wax is too cool, it tends to sit on the top layer of cloth and looks opaque. The wax should be transparent looking.

After waxing, unpin the cloth from the board and turn it over. Peel off the waxed paper. If any areas need rewaxing, lay new waxed paper on the board and repin the cloth with the front side down. Rewax the back. After waxing is completed, you are ready to dye the folded cloth.

If you use cotton dyes, follow the manufacturer's directions or directions in Project One. If you use silk dyes, follow the manufacturer's directions for the amount of acid to add to the dye, or add 1½ teaspoons glacial acetic acid to a gallon of liquid, to act as a dye fixative. Always add acid to water, not vice versa.

You can buy glacial acetic acid at chemical

Illus. 78. After the first waxing, the design is dyed while still folded.

or photo supply firms. You should have good ventilation when working with acid, as the fumes can be quite strong. Be sure to wear rubber gloves and an apron to protect yourself, as the undiluted acid can cause a severe burn. An enamelled pan makes a good dye pan.

Measure a small amount of water into a pan and heat. Dissolve the dye powder in the hot water and set aside. Measure the rest of the water needed, and pour it, lukewarm, into the dye bath container. If you are using silk dye, measure the glacial acetic acid into a glass cup, and add it to the water in the dye bath container, being careful not to breathe the fumes. Stir with a stainless steel spoon. Now add the dissolved dye and stir the dye bath again. Rinse the spoon immediately.

Dip the cloth into the dye without unfolding, and move it about gently. The folded cloth appears darker than the unfolded cloth will. To get an idea of the actual color, blot a

69

Illus. 79. Areas are filled in with wax to preserve the first color, then the batik is dyed again.

small section of a single layer dry with a paper towel. If the color is too light, leave the batik in the dye bath for a longer time. Rich or dark colors should be used, as the cloth is sheer and the design will not show unless there is contrast.

Rinse the batik until the water runs clear, and hang it to dry without unfolding. If you wish to save the dye, pour it into glass containers, and rinse the dye pan immediately. Once acid is added to the dye, the dye begins to deteriorate and will last only a day or two.

After the batik is dry, pin it to the board again for the second waxing, stretching it as smooth as possible. Use the pattern in the book as a guide, and with a brush fill in the shaded areas with wax. They are to remain the first color. For contrast, the area within the spiral is left unwaxed where the background area is waxed, and is waxed where

the background is left unwaxed. After waxing is completed, turn the batik over and retouch the back if necessary.

Dye the batik in the second color, using the same procedure as for the first color. In this scarf, red was dyed over blue, resulting in a blue, lavender, and white design.

After the second dyeing, rinse and dry the batik. Iron the folded cloth until the wax is removed, then unfold and iron again. Dry clean the cloth to make it soft; then hem the scarf.

If you want to use the design as a wall hanging, it should be backed with a white cloth before framing.

REPEAT BORDERS

Repeat borders are made in a similar way to the folded scarf design. A picture with a repeat border around it makes an interesting wall hanging or tablecloth. Organdy and voile are thin, suitable fabrics which may be dyed with household or cotton batik dyes. Organdy can only be folded in half because wax will not penetrate it as easily, but voile may be folded in fourths. Here we will use organdy.

Wax the central picture first with the cloth laid flat. Leave plenty of extra cloth all around, for the border. Dyes for the central design should be painted on, to avoid coloring the border. After the central design is completed, crease the cloth in half and pin it to a board. Wax the border design along the three unfolded edges, and paint the dye on.

After the batik is dry, carefully iron the wax out of the border only. Unfold the cloth and iron the wax out of the entire batik. The result is a central design surrounded by a symmetrical border. (See color picture on page E.)

PROJECT NINE: A MULTICOLOR HOOD

Materials

⅓ yard white cotton velveteen or fine-weave
cotton
yellow, red, and blue dyes (as close to
primary colors as possible—use household or batik dyes)
fine-spouted tjanting
alcohol lamp
brush

tape measure
non-flammable dry-cleaning solvent
scissors
newspapers and waxed paper, or frame
yardstick
1½ yards of ½-inch ribbon
pencil

This multicolor design makes an attractive beach hood when made with fine cotton, or a hood for evening when made with velveteen. Velveteen is more difficult to work with, as the thick cloth requires a triple waxing each time the design is drawn. It is waxed once to draw the design, then again on front and back for complete wax coverage. For the finished hood see color page G.

The diagrams on page 73 show two wax sequences, one to make a red hat, and one to make a green hat. Colors are repeated after every six ovals. By using solvents to completely remove the wax between each

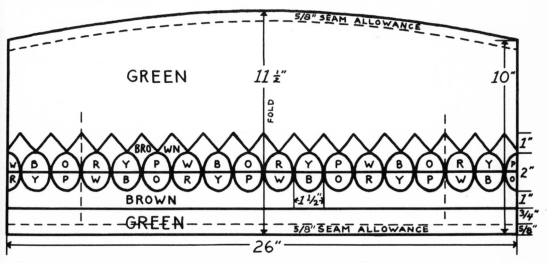

Illus. 80. Use the above pattern as a guide for making a hood. The text gives instructions for making and fitting a newspaper pattern. The oval-and-point design is dyed in a special way so you get eight colors. Color key to the oval design is: W = white, R = red, B = blue, Y = yellow, O = orange, P = purple. Six ovals make up a unit. Design begins in the middle of the hood.

dyeing, color can be added to areas that were previously covered with wax. An area that was kept white in the yellow and red dyeings, for instance, will become blue in the last dyeing. Eight colors—white, yellow, orange, red, purple, blue, green, and brown—will result from the use of yellow, red, and blue dyes. (See color pages F and G.)

The only fitting of the pattern you will need to do is for the size around your face. Use a tape measure; place it around your head where you want the front of the hood to be. Bring the ends of the tape under your chin, to find the length required. Add $2\frac{1}{2}$ inches to this length for seam allowances. The total is the length of the pattern, which is shown as 26 inches on the pattern in the book. The length of your own pattern will depend on the measurement you take as directed above and on how tight you want the hood to be around your face.

You may draw a pattern free-hand on newspaper, using the pattern in the book as a guide. (Illus. 80). Fold a piece of newspaper in half. Measure and mark off an $11\frac{1}{2}$-inch line along the fold. From the bottom end of the $11\frac{1}{2}$-inch line, draw a line at a right-angle measuring half the length you measured around your head, plus $1\frac{1}{4}$ inches. From the end of the line you have just drawn,

draw a 10-inch line parallel to the fold, so you form a three-sided box with the lines. The top of the pattern is a curved line going from the top end of the $11\frac{1}{2}$-inch line to the end of the 10-inch line. Draw this curve free-hand; then cut the pattern along the last three lines drawn on the folded newspaper. When you unfold the pattern it should be the shape of the pattern in the book.

After cutting, fit the pattern around your head, placing the front where you had previously placed the tape measure, and make any further adjustments that may be necessary. The extra cloth at the back of the neck will be gathered on a ribbon, so no pattern adjustment is necessary on this part. Wash and press the cloth before pinning and cutting the pattern.

To draw the design on the cloth, use a yardstick and a pencil to measure and draw the straight line across the bottom of the border, and the central line through the ovals. Cut a piece of paper the size of the oval pattern (Illus. 81), which is 2 inches tall by $1\frac{1}{2}$ inches wide. Starting halfway from the right edge, place the oval on the cloth, matching the central line with the line on the cloth; then trace around the oval. Move the oval pattern until it touches the edge of the first oval; then trace around it again. Repeat

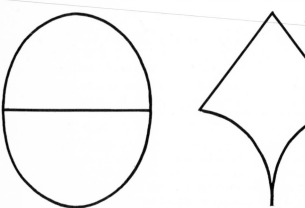

Illus. 81. These are the patterns for the oval and the point designs. Trace them directly from the book.

72

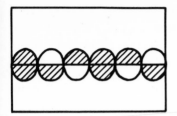
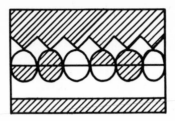
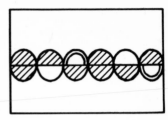

Illus. 82. Diagram for a green hood. Step 1: Wax each unit of six ovals as shown at left by shading. Dye cloth yellow. Step 2: Wax shaded areas in middle diagram as well as rest of cloth. Dye red. Step 3: Wax the ovals as shown at the right. Also draw a thin outline of wax on the half-ovals shown with a double outline. Dye blue. Finished colors will be as shown on pattern.

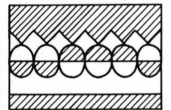
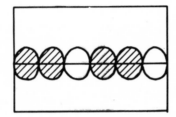
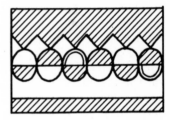

Illus. 83. Diagram for red hood. Step 1: Wax the ovals as shown at the left. Also wax rest of cloth except white areas shown. Dye yellow. Step 2: The entire cloth is left unwaxed except for the ovals shown shaded in the middle diagram. Dye red. Step 3: Wax the entire red cloth and the ovals except for the white areas in the diagram at the right. Wax the half-ovals with the double outline as for the green hood. Dye blue. When complete the ovals will be: green and white, yellow and blue, purple and orange, white and green, blue and yellow, orange and purple.

this until you have drawn a line of ovals extending to the right edge. Now draw the ovals toward the left edge until you have a line of them across the cloth. Make a pattern of the point design (Illus. 81), which extends 1 inch beyond the ovals. Place it on the cloth between a pair of ovals and trace the point, repeating until you have drawn points across the entire length of the cloth (Illus. 80).

Use the waxing diagrams (Illus. 82 and 83) as a guide to wax either a green or a red hood. The diagrams show a sequence of six

ovals. After waxing six ovals, repeat the sequence over again all along the length of the cloth. Wax as shown on the left side of the diagram for the first dyeing, as shown in the middle for the second dyeing, and as shown at the right for the third dyeing.

The sequence of dyeing is the same for both diagrams. It is the difference in the waxing that determines what colors the hood will be. You may choose either waxing diagram to follow. The left side of each diagram shows Step 1 for that hood.

To begin, use the fine tjanting to outline the areas with wax; then fill in with the tjanting or a small brush, using hot wax. If you use velveteen, you must rewax the front and back carefully with a brush, after the first layer is cool, to be sure of complete wax coverage. Avoid touching the edges with the brush as the wax may spill over on to the unwaxed areas.

After the first waxing is completed (using either diagram), wet the cloth and dye it yellow. If you have trouble wetting the velveteen before immersing it in the dye bath, add a mild detergent to the water. The cloth must be completely wet, or the dye will not take. After dyeing, hang the batik to dry, using wooden clothes-pins, or straight pins, on the corners only. The pins may cause the dye to discolor, so pin only on a seam where the marks won't show.

After the batik is dry, iron the wax out; then dry-clean the cloth to remove every trace of wax. You may have to use several changes of dry-cleaning solvent to remove all the wax. Hang to dry. Don't use plastic clothes-pins as the plastic may dissolve in the solvent.

After the solvent has completely evaporated and the cloth feels dry, wax the areas shown for Step 2 on the diagram you have chosen. Use the same waxing method as for Step 1. Dye the batik red. Be sure the cloth is completely wet before immersing it in the dye bath. Let it dry; then iron the wax out and dry-clean again.

At Step 3 in the waxing, in addition to filling in the designated areas solidly with wax, wax a thin outline around the outer edge of the areas that will become purple. The purple and brown will not contrast well, so the purple area needs an outline to set it off. Don't outline any other areas, as the other colors *will* contrast with the brown background.

Dye the batik blue. The batik will now have eight colors as a result of three dyeings. Iron the wax out and dry-clean.

To finish the hood, turn it wrong side out, fold it in half, and sew the seams along the curved side together. Turn up the seam allowance along the front of the hood and hand-sew. Turn up the raw edge at the bottom of the hood to a ¼-inch hem, and machine-stitch it. Now fold this hemmed edge, which will surround the neck, to form a ½-inch tube inside the hood for the ribbon. Place the ribbon in the tube before hand-sewing the seam. Gather the cloth along the ribbon. Adjust it to your neck size, and sew the cloth shut at each end of the tube, catching the ribbon as you sew.

See color photographs of the dyeing sequence for a green hood on pages F and G.

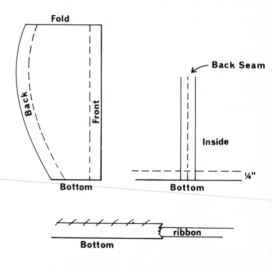

Illus. 84. First fold the cloth in half and sew the back seam on the dotted line. Make a hem by hand along the dotted line in front. Next, fold the bottom edge up on the dotted line and machine-stitch. Finally, fold the bottom edge up again to form a tube for the ribbon. Hand sew.

VARIATIONS OF BATIK

Other materials besides cloth can be decorated using a resist technique similar to that used in making cloth batiks. An example is the complexly decorated Easter eggs made in many of the Slavic countries. A wax design is drawn on the egg, which is dipped in dye, leaving an intricate pattern. Wax resist is also used to decorate ceramics. The design is painted on the clay piece with a wax emulsion, which resists the colored liquid clay painted over it. When the clay is fired (baked), the wax melts, leaving a design in the colored coating.

Paper batik is suited to the classroom as it takes few materials and is less messy than cloth batik. A wax candle, rubber cement or crayon is used as the resist. With rubber cement, the design is drawn with the cement and colored inks or watercolors are painted on the paper. The cement is rubbed off after the picture is dry.

When a white wax candle is used, all lines or areas drawn will remain white no matter what inks or watercolors are brushed over the paper to color the background. If colored crayons are used, they should harmonize with the background painted over the drawn design. Poster paints may be used over the crayon and washed off when dry, leaving a tinted background for the crayon design.

You may also use the hot-wax method to batik paper as you did cloth. Draw the design in hot wax and color the paper with alcohol-soluble wood stain. More than one color may be used by rewaxing and redyeing, proceeding from light to dark as always. The wax must be ironed out afterward in the same manner as cloth batik.

Illus. 85. Rubber cement was used as a resist; watercolor was painted over the cement.

THE TRADITIONS OF BATIK—
AN ANCIENT ART

The origin of the craft of batik is unknown, but it has been used as a method of decorating cloth for many centuries in the Orient. The first batiks were probably made in Egypt or China. From there, the craft spread to Persia, India, and other countries as populations migrated. One of the earliest preserved examples of batik, Indian screens dating from 710 to 794 A.D., show a perfection of design and symbolism that would indicate a highly developed art.

The Javanese people of Indonesia have been making batiks for hundreds of years, to be used for clothing. Among these people, the art of batik developed and became an important part of their lives. The earliest travellers to Java in the 16th century described beautiful batik work with intricate designs, over which the people worked for months to produce one piece.

Because it was against the religion of the Javanese people to paint any living creature, the batik artists stylized the design, using symbolic dots, stripes, and highly formalized birds, animals, and flowers. Certain colors and patterns were decreed by early Javanese sultans to be worn only by persons of noble

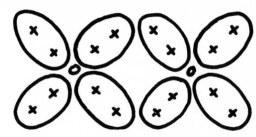

Illus. 87. A traditional kawung design.

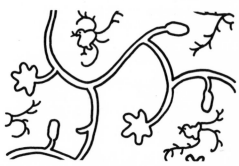

Illus. 88. Semen design shows outside influence.

birth, and some were to be worn only for official ceremonies. Batik-making was also restricted to members of the aristocracy. The secret of the technique was not well kept, however, and soon it was the hobby of every educated Javanese lady.

As more people made batiks, certain types of designs and colors came into use in different areas of the country, so one could identify the district a person came from by the clothing he wore.

There were four basic patterns of design used in classical Javanese batik. The patterns

Illus. 86. A traditional parang design.

are known as the kawung, parang, tjeplok, and semen. The kawung pattern is a group of four oval or elliptical shapes arranged so they form an overall pattern. Tiny flowers decorate the oval shapes. The parang design is formed of diagonal stripes containing stylized designs. The tjeplok pattern is a geometrical pattern of squares or circles formed from rosettes, stars or crosses, with animal or flower designs filling in the middle of the squares or circles.

The semen design shows outside influence on the basic Javanese designs, and is a freer, less geometric type of design, composed mainly of stylized shoots and leaves, with animal and flower designs filling in the background.

Toward the end of the last century, batik artists began to experiment with a greater

Illus. 89. The tjeplok pattern uses animals and flowers within squares.

Illus. 90. This batik shows a strong Chinese influence on Javanese work.

Illus. 91. Modern batiks are less stylized. Each of these animals is 6 to 8 inches long.

variety of designs, and were influenced by the tastes of outsiders, particularly the Chinese. The batiks of the early 1900's showed much inventiveness in the designs, and were much less geometric than in earlier times. Batiking is an important industry today in Indonesia, and is taught in schools to carry on a significant part of the nation's culture.

"Batik" comes from a word that means draw and write. Batiks are "written" with a tool called the tjanting, traditionally made with a copper reservoir to hold the wax, attached to a bamboo handle.

Before the Javanese woman could wax her design, she first prepared the cloth by washing it, then dipping it in a special oil to help preserve the color. Next, she removed

the excess oil, starched the cloth, and pounded it to soften the fibres. Only then was she ready to hang the cloth over a frame and begin waxing.

Holding the cloth in her left hand, she quickly dipped her tjanting in hot wax and began to trace the outlines of her design. When waxing was completed on one side of the cloth, she turned it over and retraced the design on the other side, making sure every part of the design was covered with wax. Depending on the intricacy of the design, waxing might take a number of days.

Dyeing, which was done by men, was equally painstaking, and often took several days to complete. If more than one color were planned, the batik was returned from the dyer for the woman to rewax. She re-

Illus. 92. Like all but one of the batiks in this chapter, this floral pattern is from the 1909-1935 period.

moved the first layer of wax either by boiling the cloth if all the wax was to be removed, or by sponging individual areas with hot water. The rest of the design was added on the second waxing, and the batik was sent to the dyer a second time for the final color.

The hand-drawn batik usually took at least a month to complete, and sometimes a woman would work as much as a year on an intricate design. Today, in order to shorten the process, many designs are hand-printed, using a brass stamp called the tjap to apply the wax. The hand-drawn batik is still considered the more desirable, especially if it is to be worn on important occasions. With modern techniques, however, it is difficult to tell the difference between a carefully printed batik and a hand-drawn one that has a geometric design.

American batik has been greatly modified from the traditional painstaking designs of the Javanese. This does not mean that modern batiks show no craftsmanship.

Modern batiks need to be planned according to the use of the batiked object. Some designs may take a great deal of skill; others are simpler to make. By using the basic techniques of batik in new ways, we can enjoy a creative hobby that can change as styles change, to make beautiful decorations for our homes.

Illus. 93. Basically geometrical, this batik was made circa 1840.

INDEX